RE FEB 2013

D0402316

Thunderbird Spirit

Sigmund Brouwer

orca sports

ORCA BOOK PUBLISHERS

Copyright © 2008 Sigmund Brouwer

All rights reserved. No part of this publication may be reproduced
or transmitted in any form or by any means, electronic or mechanical, including
photocopying, recording or by any information storage
and retrieval system now known or to be invented, without permission
in writing from the publisher.

Library and Archives Canada Cataloguing in Publication

Brouwer, Sigmund, 1959-
Thunderbird spirit / written by Sigmund Brouwer.

(Orca sports)
ISBN 978-1-55469-045-9

I. Title. II. Series.
PS8553.R68467T486 2008   jc813'.54   c2008-903424-4

First published in the United States, 2008
Library of Congress Control Number: 2008930033

Summary: Spin-off racial hatred takes hockey players
Keats and Dakota into a web of violence and deceit that makes
winning this year's league title the least of their concerns.

Orca Book Publishers gratefully acknowledges the support for its publishing
programs provided by the following agencies: the Government of Canada through
the Canada Book Fund and the Canada Council for the Arts,
and the Province of British Columbia through the BC Arts Council
and the Book Publishing Tax Credit.

Cover design by Bruce Collins
Cover photography by Getty Images
Author photo by Bill Bilsley

ORCA BOOK PUBLISHERS
PO Box 5626, Stn. B
Victoria, BC Canada
V8R 6S4

ORCA BOOK PUBLISHERS
PO Box 468
Custer, WA USA
98240-0468

www.orcabook.com
Printed and bound in Canada.
Printed on 100% PCW recycled paper.

13 · 12 11 10 • 5 4 3 2

chapter one

"Keats, you boneheaded jerk!" The voice came from above me, at the top of the Plexiglas surrounding the penalty box. The guy sounded like he was using a megaphone. I could hear him clearly above the thousands of yelling fans, who were glad to see me get a penalty here in Saskatoon.

The score was 3-3 with only five minutes left in the hockey game. The center on my line, Dakota Smith, was already in the penalty box. With me beside him, it left five of their Saskatoon Blades against three of our Seattle Thunderbirds. Worse, the Blades were only one game behind us in the overall league standings. We needed this win to stay in first place going into the playoffs.

"You hear me, Keats?" the voice screamed again.

I ignored him. I spend a lot of time in the penalty box, and I get yelled at a lot by angry hockey fans. I expected Saskatoon fans to hate me.

"You're a boneheaded jerk!" he hollered. "Play hockey instead of running people into the boards!"

I could have told him I'm one of the smallest guys on the ice. Can I help it if bigger players trip over my knee and smash into the boards? But the referee hadn't believed my story. This guy probably wouldn't either. Besides, he wasn't getting to me. I've been called worse things than a boneheaded jerk.

"How about you, redskin?" the guy yelled at my teammate beside me. "Where's your bow and arrow?"

Now I was mad. I'd only been on the Seattle Thunderbirds two weeks, and Dakota Smith kept to himself, so it wasn't like we had become friends. I didn't know much about him, but I did know he was definitely Native North American. He was tall and big-shouldered. He had long black hair, high cheekbones and skin like unpolished copper.

I turned and half stood. "That's enough, bozo!" I yelled. Bow and arrow was going well past what fans should be allowed to say.

Dakota pulled me back down to a sitting position.

"Don't sweat it," Dakota told me calmly, still staring straight ahead. "This happens all the time."

I twisted my head and glared at the fan. He was leaning halfway over the Plexiglas, just above me. He had long greasy hair and wore a dirty denim jacket with a black T-shirt underneath. He was so close I could see the hairs growing out of his nostrils.

"Bozo, Keats? Bozo?" he shouted, working himself into a frenzy. "You're both losers! A crazy man and an Indian chief! Clear the rink before we clear you!"

Dakota stayed calm, and it helped me keep my temper. Instead of yelling something, I managed to force myself to smile sweetly into the screaming guy's face.

That just made him angrier. He started shouting so loud that drool slid out the sides of his mouth. When I realized my smile drove him nuts, I just kept smiling.

"Aargh!" he shouted, waving his arms. "Aargh!" He was so mad he couldn't even find words anymore.

I kept smiling.

"Aargh!" he shouted again. Then he leaned down even farther. And he spit right into my face.

The guys on the team tell me that when I go crazy, my eyeballs roll back into my head. If that's true, my eyeballs were spinning in circles as I wiped the spit off my cheek. And I lost it. Totally.

Without thinking, without caring, I reached up and grabbed the guy by the shoulders of his denim jacket. I yanked him face down into the penalty box.

I made one mistake. I pulled too hard.

When I lose my temper, I sometimes forget my own strength. I pulled so hard that the guy slid right across the lap of my slippery nylon hockey pants. His face ended up in Dakota's lap.

I couldn't hear the crowd, of course, because when I lose my temper, nothing gets through. Later the guys told me the crowd went totally crazy too: Screaming. Yelling. Cheering. I also later learned that the referee had noticed and had blown the whistle to stop play and to call for security guards.

All I knew was I wanted to get this guy for calling Dakota names and for spitting in my face.

But I couldn't. Not with his face and shoulders across Dakota's lap. Not with Dakota calmly pinning the guy's arms so he couldn't fight.

When I looked down, all I could see was the backs of his legs, the back of the top of his pants and the back of the bottom of his jacket. Mad as I was, I wasn't going to start spanking the guy.

I had to do something to punish this guy. Just when I thought my body would pop like a balloon from anger, I saw it. Where his jacket and black T-shirt had lifted to show some skin, I saw the top of the guy's underwear.

I grabbed it with one hand. Then with the other. And I pulled as hard as I could. I didn't stop yanking upward until his underwear almost reached his shoulder blades.

He screamed and yelled and squirmed. Dakota held him to keep him from turning over and swinging at either of us. And I kept pulling, even when my arms felt so tired I almost had to let go. Right about then, the security guards got to the penalty box.

I was glad to let go, so they could haul the guy out of there. While I don't lose my temper terribly often, when I do, I really flare. It came and went so fast that I was already feeling embarrassed by what I had done.

The security guards led the fan up the stairs away from the penalty box, one on each side so he wouldn't try to get away. But I don't think he felt like running. Because when I looked over my shoulder to watch him walk up the stairs of the ice rink, the top of his underwear was still halfway up his back.

"Well, Mike," Dakota said to me above the insane roaring of the crowd, "I can see how you got your nickname."

chapter two

Getting called into the coach's office is like getting called into the principal's office. And I never have good enough grades to hope it's because the principal has nice news.

"Yes, Coach?" I didn't step all the way inside. Maybe he wanted to speak to someone else. Maybe our trainer had called the wrong person from the dressing room down the hallway. Or maybe I was going to be traded. Again.

"Michael," Coach Nesbitt said, "come in."

He didn't call me Mike. Or Keats. I had a bad feeling about this.

"Sure, Coach."

He pointed me to a chair in the corner. I sat down.

On a shelf behind his desk were trophies and hockey photos. One photo showed Coach Nesbitt with Wayne Gretzky at a golf tournament. Wayne was taller and skinnier. The photo was a few years old. Coach Nesbitt had less hair now, and what was left of his hair was salt-and-pepper gray.

"I want you to think about Saskatoon," he said.

I nearly laughed a sad laugh. When didn't I think about Saskatoon?

Saskatoon, Saskatchewan.

Already, after only two weeks in Seattle, I wished I had a goal for every time someone asked me to repeat those two words after my explaining I used to play there.

Saskatoon, Saskatchewan.

People in Seattle smile when I say it, like they think I still talk baby talk. I've even had a few say, "Bless you," as if I had just sneezed.

Then I have to explain that Saskatoon is a city with a Western Hockey League team, and that Saskatchewan is not a sneeze but the Canadian province right above North Dakota.

Actually, Saskatoon people are crazy about hockey, and it is a great city for hockey players. But only if you wear a Saskatoon Blades uniform. For a player on any other team in the WHL, the Saskatoon ice arena is not a great place to be.

Saskatoon is bad enough for other out-of-town players. For me, it was horrible. I had left the Saskatoon Blades under bad terms. In leaving, I'd also left behind the closest thing to family I'd ever had.

Coach Nesbitt snapped me from my thoughts. "We need to discuss what happened in Saskatoon," he said.

It hung there while I kept my face stiff and stared back at him. Some labels are bad enough: Troublemaker. Bad-tempered. Rebel. I could live with those. I deserved them. Other labels—like thief—hurt worse and follow you longer. I had not defended myself in Saskatoon. I sure wasn't going to start now.

He realized what he'd just said. "I don't mean why they traded you. I mean the penalty-box incident."

I nodded. I'd been wondering when he would get around to this. It had been four days since I'd lost my temper in the Saskatoon penalty box. We had played other teams on three of those days. We'd tied the Regina Pats the day after Saskatoon and lost to the Red Deer Rebels the next day. Then we killed the Lethbridge Hurricanes, leaving us a full day to get home to Seattle by bus. I'd been dreading this moment all that time.

"Saskatoon was great, wasn't it?" I said. "Remember how we killed off that two-man penalty and then pulled off a win in over-time against the Blades?" I snapped my fingers. "Wow! Now that I think of it, I did score that overtime goal, didn't I?"

It had been a beauty. Their defenseman had slapped a cross-ice pass right onto my stick, and I had burned up the ice on a breakaway, pulling the goalie left, flipping the puck to my backhand and firing the puck high into the right corner of the net. Yes, it had been dumb taking a penalty. It had been even worse to lose my temper when the guy spit in my face. At least, though, I'd scored the winning goal.

Coach Nesbitt buried his face in his hands. I heard him let out a deep sigh.

"Yes, we did win," he said when he pulled his hands away. "And, yes, you did score."

I grinned. I doubted my happy grin was fooling either of us, but I figured it couldn't hurt to try.

"I also remember a few other things," Coach said. "I remember you throwing someone into the boards and taking a penalty when Dakota was already in the box. That was a bad time to put us deeper in the hole."

"The guy hacked my ribs with his hockey stick," I protested. "I couldn't let him get away with—"

"How many times have coaches had to talk to you about this?" Coach Nesbitt interrupted.

"I don't know," I said. "I score lots of goals, but not too many in overtime."

He slammed his fist on his desk. It shook the coffee mug that held his pens and pencils.

"Quit clowning, Keats. You know exactly what I mean." He glared at me. "And I want you to tell me exactly what I mean. Right now."

I examined the tops of my knees. I hadn't had a chance to change into my hockey gear yet, so I was still in blue jeans. There was a hole just above my left knee. A small hole. I knew it would get bigger though. I'd probably have to buy a new pair soon and—

"Keats, lift your head! At least have the guts to look me in the eye."

I lifted my head and glared back at Coach Nesbitt. "You want to talk to me about how I lose control when I lose my temper," I told him. "I need to learn to curb it, so I can reach my potential as a hockey player."

Coach Nesbitt settled back in his chair and sighed again. "I wish you knew how sad it makes me to watch someone as good as you throw it all away."

I went back to staring at the tiny hole just above the left knee of my jeans.

"Come on, Keats," he said. "I want to help."

"That guy made some crack to Dakota about a bow and arrow, Coach. He spit in my face. What was I supposed to do?"

"Not try to rip his underwear off, that's for sure." Coach Nesbitt chuckled at the memory and then remembered I was in front of him. He forced a frown back on his face. "Dakota told me what happened, Keats. He told me you shouldn't be blamed. I have a lot of respect for Dakota, and I'm going to go on his word. I've written a report and sent it to the league's head office, requesting that you not be fined or suspended."

"Is that why you called me here?" I grinned again. This was the first time in a while that getting called to the coach's office had meant good news.

"It's only part of the reason." His frown deepened. "Keats, the Seattle Thunderbirds may be your last stop. In three years, you've played for four teams. We both know why you had to leave Saskatoon. If we don't keep you, I doubt anyone will pick you up. And you know what it means if you can't play in the WHL."

It meant I'd never have a chance at getting drafted into the National Hockey League. The WHL was the last step before making a pro team. I'd been dreaming about that since I was a kid.

I picked at the hole in my jeans.

"Look," Coach Nesbitt said, "I'm on your side. I know you had it tough growing up. I really want to help you."

15

I stood, walked up to his desk and put my hands on it. I leaned forward and looked him straight in the eyes. My voice was tight with anger. "Two things, Coach Nesbitt. One, you have no idea what growing up was like for me. Nobody can. And two, it's none of your business. Ever."

He pushed his chair back and stood. We were the same height. I was a short hockey player. He was a short coach.

"Two things, Michael Keats." His voice sounded as angry as mine. "One, you're right. It is none of my business. And two, speak to me like that again and you're suspended for ten games."

He stared at me, daring me to say anything else.

I wanted to. Then I thought of how much I still wanted to play hockey. I thought of Dakota Smith and how cool he had been when the guy in Saskatoon mouthed off about a bow and arrow.

"I'll try to watch my temper," I said.

"Good. Now get back to the dressing room and get ready for practice." He allowed me a small smile. "You guys had a great road trip, and I'm going to skate the team easy today."

I walked out of there with my jaw shut tight.

I was still mad when I got to the dressing room. Most of the guys were already in their equipment and on the ice, which was good. I didn't feel like talking. I hated it when anything or anyone reminded me why I had been forced to leave Saskatoon.

chapter three

Coach Nesbitt lived up to his promise. It was a light practice. He ended it after only an hour. By then, of course, I was in a better mood.

I showered and dressed in a hurry because I wanted to catch Dakota Smith. He was usually the first guy out of the dressing room, and he never hung around the rink with the rest of the team.

When I got out to the parking lot, I had to pull my collar up against the drizzle. Gray fog draped across the dark green of the high hills around us. People in Seattle told me it was always like this in February. I didn't mind the drizzle, though, or the fog. It sure beat the cold weather up in Saskatoon.

The big parking lot around the arena held very few cars. I jumped over puddles as I ran to catch up to Dakota. I still had to shout his name to keep him from getting into his truck before I reached him.

During my two weeks with the Seattle Thunderbirds, I hadn't heard Dakota Smith speak more than a dozen words. He always sat by himself on the bus on road trips, reading thick books. It wasn't that he was a nerd. Or that he couldn't have friends. It was more like we were so unsure of him that we kept our distance. He had a reputation as someone you didn't want to mess with. While Dakota Smith was probably only seventeen, just like me, he carried himself as if he were a legendary warrior of a fierce noble tribe.

Dakota could play. He was fast, sweeping through the opposing teams like wind through pine trees. He was smooth, like a mountain river flowing over round boulders. And he had a shot as deadly as a striking snake.

"Dakota!" I shouted again as I hurried.

He leaned against his truck and waited for me. I knew what I wanted to say but not how to say it.

"Nice truck," I said when I got there.

He grunted.

We both knew it wasn't a nice truck. It was an old Dodge 4x4. Green. Banged up. Splattered with caked-on mud that was probably older than most cars.

I shrugged. "Actually, it's an ugly truck."

For the first time ever, I saw him grin. "Yup. But it will get me anywhere."

"Look," I said, "I just want to thank you for helping me with Coach Nesbitt. He used your story on a report. I probably won't get suspended."

"No problem," Dakota said.

I noticed neither of us talked about how the guy had taunted him. Actually, I noticed neither of us said much of anything. I'd never been good at thanking people.

"Well," I said, "that's it, I guess. Thanks."

He nodded and opened his truck door. I figured that meant the end of our conversation.

I turned away. I didn't take another step though.

Another 4x4 truck was heading straight toward us, spraying water as it ripped through puddles.

The driver was an idiot. If he didn't slow down soon, he'd crash straight into Dakota's truck.

Dakota stepped away from his truck.

"What's that idiot—?" I never had a chance to finish my question.

The red 4x4 spun sideways as the driver slammed on the brakes and yanked the steering wheel. The truck skidded toward Dakota's truck. I couldn't see the driver because the passenger side was sliding

21

toward us. I could see the passenger though. He wore a mask over his face. And he was pointing a rifle at us through the open window.

Dakota dove into me and sent us sprawling into a puddle.

I heard a sharp crack, then a roar as the truck took off.

Cold water soaked my jeans and my jacket. I rolled away from Dakota and helped him to his feet.

"Those guys were nuts!"

Dakota didn't answer. He stared at the windshield of his truck. I saw what he saw. And I didn't like it.

On the left side of the windshield, right above the steering wheel, was a small dark hole. And I could see a bigger hole in the back window. Both were caused by the same thing: a bullet. A bullet that would have taken Dakota's head off if he had been sitting behind the steering wheel.

chapter four

"Come on!" I shouted. At the far end of the parking lot, the red 4x4 was disappearing in a big spray of water.

I raced to the other side of Dakota's truck and jumped inside. I pounded against the dash in excitement. Nobody could take a rifle shot in our direction and get away with it.

But Dakota did not jump behind the steering wheel. Instead he slowly walked around to my side of the truck.

I rolled down the window and looked up at him. "They're getting away, man. Let's get moving!"

Dakota leaned against the outside mirror of the truck and looked down at me.

"You are crazy," he said. His long dark hair was fanned against his shoulders. The drizzle made his face look like it was sweating.

"Crazy? Everyone knows that's my nickname."

"I mean you truly are a crazy person. Those guys have a rifle."

"So?" I asked.

"Lift your hands," he told me.

I did.

"I don't see a rifle," he said. "What are you going to do if we catch them? Throw rocks? Bite their kneecaps?"

"And you're going to stand there and let them get away with shooting at you?"

"Actually, they shot at my truck," he said. "Big difference."

"They shot at your truck," I repeated. "That's all? It's not like they hit it with a snowball."

Dakota shrugged. As if they had hit it with a snowball.

"You're the crazy one," I said. "You should be yelling. Getting mad. Chasing them. Calling the cops. Not just standing there."

He shrugged again. I shook my head. I mean, how cool should a person be in a situation like this?

"Dakota," I said, "it's not like people shoot at trucks every day."

"No?" There was a sad smile on his face.

I saw his eyes look down at the outside of the door. I followed his gaze. A few inches away from the door handle—on the inside of the door—was a hole barely wider than a pencil.

"What?" I shoved the door open, pushing Dakota away from the truck. I stared at the outside of the door. Sure enough, on the outside too, there was a matching hole.

I put my pinkie finger in it, feeling the sharp edges where a bullet had torn through the metal.

"It's been shot before." This was making me dizzy.

"Look," Dakota said, "I'm sorry you had to get involved. Just forget about it, okay?"

I shook my head. "Let me get this straight. Someone just shot at you. And—"

"Someone shot at my truck. I told you. Big difference."

"And it's not the first time. And you want me to pretend nothing has happened."

"There are only five games left before playoffs," he said. "If people find out about this, there will be police and newspaper reporters. I just want to be left alone so I can play hockey."

"Are the people who shot at you going to leave you alone?"

"The people shot at my truck. Remember?"

"You're insane. What if you're in your truck next time they shoot?" I kicked the front tire.

He grinned when I started hopping around and yelling at my foot. It felt like I had broken a couple of toes.

"Mike," he said, "I like you. Do me a favor and don't worry about this."

"Why not?"

"Because after next Sunday, there won't be a reason for anyone to get in my face anymore."

I stared at him. "Sure," I finally promised. "I won't worry about this."

"Or tell anyone."

"Sure." At least this promise would be easier to keep than the first one. I was used to not telling people things.

Dakota dug his truck keys from his pocket. Walking around the front of the truck, he opened the door on the driver's side. He dusted the broken glass off the seat before sliding behind the steering wheel.

I kept staring at him. This was an unbelievable situation. It sounded like he knew exactly who had shot at him.

What was going on? Why were they shooting at him? Why didn't he go crazy about it? And how did he know when it was going to end?

I realized I'd already broken my first promise by beginning to worry about him.

As Dakota started his truck, the exhaust pipe burped a cloud of blue smoke. He drove off, leaving me to stare at the back of his beat-up green truck.

The brake lights came on. Then the reverse lights. He backed up until he was beside me. He rolled down his window and leaned on the door as he looked at me.

"Mike," he said.

"Yeah?"

"You might want to remember we landed in a puddle when I dove into you."

"I remember." I was soaked pretty good because of it.

"Well, you should change your pants," he said. "You look like you wet yourself."

With a grin, he drove away.

chapter five

The next day we had a game against the Winter Hawks in Portland. The bus was scheduled to leave the rink at two o'clock in the afternoon. I got there early and parked my car—an old, rusty, gray Toyota Corolla—near the cars of the other guys who had arrived ahead of me.

As I waited with them next to the team bus, I kept watching for Dakota's green truck to come chugging into the parking lot. I was worried about him, and I hoped nothing had happened to him overnight. It got to the point where I almost told Coach Nesbitt about the bullet holes, but I remembered my promise to Dakota and managed to keep my mouth shut.

When Dakota finally arrived, I took a deep breath. He parked the truck away from the rest of the players' cars and nodded at me as he joined us.

When something else grabbed Dakota's attention, I took a good look at his truck.

No new bullet holes.

That, at least, was good news, even if I was going nuts trying to figure out what was happening to him. The night before, while falling asleep, I'd even wondered if Dakota were part of a drug ring or something. After all, maybe he didn't want to go to the police because he was more scared of the police than of the guys shooting at him.

I had stared at the ceiling, though, and told myself that there had to be another reason. Dakota wasn't the kind of guy to do anything stupid. But I couldn't come up with any other reason for what was happening.

At exactly two o'clock, Coach Nesbitt waved us onto the bus. Dakota took his usual seat near the front, and as usual he opened up a book. It seemed like he didn't want to talk to me, so I sat in the back of the bus with a couple of guys who always sat back there and listened to all the same dumb jokes we told on every bus trip.

A few hours later, we crossed the Columbia River and hit the outside suburbs of Portland.

The mood in the bus changed as we began to think about the game ahead of us.

We wanted to win for a bunch of reasons. Every game we played this late in the season was important. Although we were in first place and were guaranteed to finish as one of the top three teams, we didn't want to get into a losing streak as the playoffs approached.

As well, it made a big difference to us whether we finished first, second or third. If we finished at the top of the overall standings, we could expect to play the weakest team in our first-round playoff games. The easier our first round of playoff games, the better we would do as the playoffs continued. On the other hand, finishing second or third would give us much tougher opponents once the playoffs started.

Finally, there was the traditional rivalry against Portland. Even though I was a new player to the team, I'd heard a lot about the rivalry when I played for other teams in the WHL. This rivalry meant that even if Seattle was in last place instead of first place, we would still hate to lose to Portland—almost as much as they hated losing to us. Knowing Portland hated losing to us, of course, made it that much sweeter to beat them. Especially in their own building.

The game started off slowly. The Winter Hawks kept dumping the puck into our end and chasing it. Our defense safely moved the puck up along the boards, and we forwards dumped the puck into the Winter Hawks' end and chased it.

Back and forth. Back and forth. Our end, then theirs. To the fans, it was probably like watching a Ping-Pong ball instead of a puck.

Zero to zero at the end of the first.

Two to two at the end of the second.

Midway through the third period, our line—me, Dakota Smith and Randy Kowerski—stepped onto the ice. We did a good job of forechecking the Winter Hawks, and it took them nearly a minute to get the puck out of their zone.

Randy chased their center, who was taking the puck across center ice. Sweeping his stick in a big circle, Randy tried to knock the puck off their center's stick. The Winter Hawks center stepped on the blade of Randy's stick and fell to his knees.

The puck squirted to me. I had open ice and saw a good chance to bust past their defenseman. But as soon as I touched the puck, the referee blew his whistle.

"What!" I screamed.

The referee didn't answer. He pointed at Randy Kowerski and motioned a tripping penalty.

"What?" I yelled again. "Bad call, ref!" I skated toward him. Normally only the captain or assistant captains can talk to the ref. But this ref had not only called a dumb penalty, he'd also stopped me from a good scoring chance.

People in the stands booed me. I ignored them. I'd been booed plenty before.

"Really bad call, ref!" I yelled at the ref's back and shoulders as I tried to catch up. "That guy stepped on Randy's stick!"

The referee didn't look my way. Maybe I hadn't yelled loud enough. After all, this crowd was raising the roof of the building with noise. Some of the fans were even standing to shake their fists at me as they booed.

"Get thicker glasses, you blind bat!" I shouted. "There're two teams out here! Not just ours!"

The referee still ignored me.

"Hey, ref!" I screamed.

He finally started skating back toward me.

"Yeah, you!" I shouted. "You're the biggest idio—"

Before I could finish telling him what I thought of his lack of brain power, Dakota yanked me backward. I almost fell.

I was still trying to pull myself loose from Dakota's grip when the referee reached me.

He stuck his head close to mine. He had a goofy big nose and eyes that looked like marbles behind the thick lenses of his glasses.

"Keats, did you have something to say?" the ref asked. His voice was low and angry.

"I sure did," I said. "Do you have a driver's license?"

He frowned. "Yes."

"Be careful out there. Because blind people—"

I nearly choked on the fingers of the hockey glove Dakota suddenly shoved into my mouth.

"He has often told me the same, sir," Dakota said to the referee as he pushed the glove deeper into my throat. "My teammate feels much sympathy for the visually challenged. I will remind him, however, that a hockey game is not the time or place for this type of discussion."

The referee stared at Dakota, trying to figure out if he was serious. I couldn't see Dakota's face, because I was too busy trying to get my mouth unstuffed.

The referee looked at me. "Mgghhhffthh," I said. It is hard to say "idiot" when your tongue can't move.

Finally the referee shook his head in disgust at the both of us and skated away.

Dakota took his glove out of my mouth.

"Visually challenged?" I gasped, trying to get air. Fans kept booing me. "Visually challenged! What kind of thing is that to say!"

"It means blind," Dakota said. "And we don't need you to get us another penalty for yelling at the referee."

I spit out tiny pieces of leather. I drew a breath to tell Dakota what I thought of him minding my business.

"Settle down, Mike," he warned. "Learn to adjust to the situation instead of letting the situation control you."

I stared into his dark eyes. He didn't flinch or look away. Finally I nodded. Slowly.

Dakota grinned. "Now, let's get serious about killing this penalty."

chapter six

There were four of us against five Winter Hawks skaters.

They pressed us hard for the first minute of the penalty, taking at least seven good shots on our goalie.

The puck slid behind our net. Their right winger chased it hard. I followed him partway but hung back in case he decided to pass it to their defenseman.

The right winger took the puck out the other side, so I drifted even closer to the Winter Hawks defenseman on my side of the ice. I needed to guard him so he wouldn't be able to take a clear shot at the net.

Their right winger passed the puck up the boards to the defenseman, Eric Smedley, on the other side of the ice.

I got ready and watched Smedley closely. He was a big mean player with braces on his teeth. He liked to throw his elbows into any face within reach. That made him a hard guy to forget.

Earlier in the game, I had noticed something else about Smedley: Whenever he was going to pass the puck one way, he'd first fake a pass the other way.

He had the puck now, high near our blue line. Dakota, on the other side of the ice, cruised toward Smedley. Dakota didn't commit himself to rushing at Smedley, because Smedley could easily pass the puck down the boards into our corner. Or he could pass across to the other defenseman or take a shot at the net. No way could Dakota cover all three options.

Dakota moved closer. Smedley made the little stick move to fake a pass back down the boards into our corner. If I was right, that meant he was going to pass across to the defenseman on my side.

I acted on instinct, hoping I'd guessed right.

I jumped forward, diving flat on my belly for the open ice between both defensemen. If I'd guessed wrong, I was dead. My dive would take me out of the play, leaving my side of the ice totally unguarded. It was such a risky play, I was probably going to get in trouble even if it worked.

But I'm used to being in trouble.

I dove, stretching my stick flat on the ice as far ahead of me as I could reach.

I'd guessed right. Smedley ended his fake pass with a pass to the defenseman on my side of the ice.

I still wasn't safe though. If Smedley flipped the puck into the air, over my stretched-out stick, I would be as dead as if I'd guessed wrong.

But he passed the puck flat on the ice. It smacked my stick and rolled away from my sliding face.

My first goal had been to block the pass. That's all. Stop the play and get the puck out past our blue line into the safety of center ice.

Now I saw a new chance. The puck was bouncing ahead of me. If I could get to my feet fast enough...

Smedley was racing toward me to make up for his mistake.

I was already scrambling onto my knees, knocking the puck well ahead of both of us with the blade of my stick.

As Smedley reached me, I was on my skates, busting for the puck.

There were seven skaters behind us at the far end. Only their goalie was ahead of us. The one thing in all that open ice was a small black puck, wobbling on the center line, waiting like a reward.

Shorter legs like mine usually mean faster legs, at least in sprinting. My skates were a blur, and I slowly edged away from

Smedley. I got the puck on my stick and put my head down to get extra speed. But I couldn't relax. Too soon Smedley with his longer legs would start to catch me. I crossed the blue line and reached the top of the face-off circles. I felt Smedley's stick hook around my waist.

The goalie braced himself in the net. Twice tonight I'd had good chances in close, and twice I'd tried stickhandling around him. Did he think I'd try a shot this time?

Smedley was almost on me. I didn't have time to worry. I snapped a low screamer, aiming for the goalie's glove side, hoping he'd have a tough time reaching down for it.

I caught him by surprise. The red light behind the net flipped on as the net behind the goalie bulged from the force of the puck. Three to two for us!

The Winter Hawks crowd moaned.

I raised my hands in victory and skated back to the players' box.

Dakota skated alongside me. "A little more fun than watching the game from the penalty box?"

"Yes, Mom," I said.

He slapped my back and returned my grin.

The guys gave me high fives as I stepped inside. A shorthanded goal is a big boost anytime. It's even better late in a tie game against the Winter Hawks.

I moved farther along the bench, puffing and sweating. When the guys finished slapping my back, Coach Nesbitt stepped close to me.

"Keats," he said, "that was a risky move. If it hadn't worked, you'd be walking back to Seattle. As it is, I don't know whether to shake your hand or bench you."

I pulled my hand loose from my hockey glove and held it out, grinning and hoping.

He grinned back and shook my hand.

We ended up winning 3-2, and we celebrated all the way back to Seattle—until the bus pulled into the parking lot.

As we drove around the front of the ice arena, we were greeted by the flashing red and blue and yellow lights of police cars and fire trucks.

All of the players crowded toward the bus windows, straining to see what was going on. When we pulled up to where we had parked our cars earlier in the day, we discovered what had happened.

Dakota Smith's ugly green truck was no longer green. It was black. Not from a new paint job. But from fire. His truck had become a smoke-filled, burned-out wreck.

That wasn't even the worst of it.

The bus stopped well short of the fire trucks, and we tumbled out the front door.

The police had already set up barricades. We got as close as we could, talking in low excited tones about something too difficult to believe.

When we got to the barricade, we all shut our mouths. The night air was filled with the rumbling of diesel engines and the static of emergency radios. But not one of our voices added to the noise when we saw why the truck had been roped off by the police.

In big, white, spray-painted letters on the pavement around the truck was a simple message: *GO BACK TO YOUR TRIBE OR DIE IN THE CITY.*

chapter seven

"How about a ride home?" I offered Dakota. The rest of the players had left long ago. Coach Nesbitt was talking to a cop. I'd been waiting in my Toyota listening to country music for the last half hour while other cops asked Dakota questions about his truck.

"What's that?" Dakota turned his head toward me. He stared at me as if I had just appeared out of the red and yellow lights swirling through the drizzle and darkness.

To Dakota, I guess, it probably seemed like I had. I doubt he had heard me walk over from my car, and I had needed to tap his shoulder to get his attention away from the ruins of his 4x4.

"Need a ride?" I repeated.

"Coach Nesbitt said he'd take me home."

"Coach Nesbitt," I said, "will ask all the same questions that you just lied about to the cops."

Dakota's hair was tied back in a pony-tail. He tilted his head and studied me. The outline of his face reminded me of the way an eagle might stare. Then I saw a gleam of white from the dark shadows of his face. He was grinning at me.

"Mike," he said, "why would you think I've just lied to the police?"

"Like you're going to tell them someone shot at you twice? And that you somehow forgot to report it?"

"Good point," he said.

"I'll bet you told them you had no idea what any of this was about."

"Good guess. I told them that someone must really hate my red skin." He shrugged and grinned again. "Although it's really more like a nice dark suntan. Only I don't have to pay to use a fancy tanning bed."

I knew enough about hiding pain to see that his joke wasn't really a joke.

"Good thing the truck is so burned they won't notice the bullet holes," I said, doing my best to change the subject.

"Yeah, good thing," he said. "Why didn't I think of burning it myself?"

I had to laugh.

When I got quiet again, Dakota spoke. "So, Mike," he said, "how do you know that Coach Nesbitt will ask all the same questions as the police?"

"I've had people give me rides home, just so they can ask me questions. You can't jump out of a moving car and walk away if you don't like the questions."

"Oh."

I regretted what I'd said. Coach Nesbitt had put in a good word for me, had kept me from being suspended. "I didn't mean that,"

I said. "Coach is a nice guy. He cares about his players. Of course he's going to ask you questions."

"How about you?" Dakota said. "You saw the bullet holes. You know what happened yesterday in the parking lot. What are you going to ask me as you drive me home?"

"In case you haven't noticed," I said, "I've got enough troubles of my own. The only thing I'll ask you about is directions."

chapter eight

I kept my word. I didn't ask Dakota a single question about the guys who had shot at his truck. I didn't ask if he thought they were the same guys who had burned his truck. I didn't ask why someone would be doing this to him. I didn't ask why he wanted to hide what he knew about them from the police. I didn't ask how he knew it would all stop next Sunday. I didn't ask if he was afraid. I didn't ask if he wanted help.

I only asked for directions.

We got onto Interstate 5 and took it to Route 520, toward the floating bridge on Lake Washington. Before we reached the bridge, however, Dakota told me to go north. I followed signs directing us toward the University of Washington.

I'd heard of this area—Madison Park—on the west shore of Lake Washington. It was a place for millionaires' mansions. I didn't say anything though. If Dakota wanted to take a shortcut, I wasn't going to argue with him. As we drove in silence, the drizzling rain stopped. When my windshield wipers began to squeak on dry windows, I shut them off. Every few minutes, Dakota told me to make a turn to the right or to the left.

We climbed over the hill. Seattle was on the other side. Houses got bigger as we rose higher into the subdivisions. Occasionally, breaks between the houses gave us a great view of the university lights and the lake below.

Finally I stopped where Dakota told me I should let him out of the car. I winced at the clanking of gears and at the chugging of my leaky muffler. Normally it didn't bother me to drive such an old clunker. But from the size of the houses along these streets, it felt like I was breaking the law just by driving my car into the neighborhood.

The streetlights gave me enough light to see exactly how nice these mansions were. They were all three- and four-story houses, looking as big as churches. Long tree-lined driveways led up to each house. Huge windows—dark at this hour—overlooked huge yards.

"Fancy part of town," I said. "How did you luck into staying with a family around here?"

"I was born in the right hospital at the right time," Dakota said. He said it so quietly, I didn't know whether I had heard him right.

"Huh?" I said. In the WHL, when you moved to a different town, the team arranged for you to stay with host families. These were known as billets. The team paid them for rent and some grocery money.

But billets don't host hockey players to make money, because we eat a lot of groceries. Instead billet families usually love hockey and want to help out. My new billets were exactly like that. A dad and mom and three boys still in elementary school. They were nice to me, but they certainly didn't live in a mansion. And I couldn't figure out what being born in the right hospital at the right time had to do with ending up with billets who lived in a million-dollar house.

"The right hospital at the right time," Dakota said again. He still spoke quietly. I had to listen hard to catch each word. "When I was born, I ended up going home with the people who live here."

"Huh? What happened to your parents?"

By the way Dakota froze and stared straight ahead, I knew I had said something wrong. But I couldn't figure out what. For a couple of seconds, there was only the chugging of my car's muffler. I half expected every window in the neighborhood to suddenly light up as people got out of bed to see the cause of such an uncivilized noise. I shut the engine off.

More silence. This was not good.

"I don't get it," I said. "What's the matter?"

"You probably wouldn't get it." I heard rare anger in his voice. "But then, no one has called you a redskin. Or worse."

"Huh?"

"Look," he said, "you saw those words spray-painted around my truck." He laughed. It sounded bitter. "'Go back to your tribe.'"

"Yeah, I saw the writing. I thought it was ignorant. If I ever get hold of the guy who did it, I'll punch his lights out."

"Punching his lights out wouldn't solve anything," Dakota said, still staring straight ahead at the wide paved street in front of us. "You can't change people like that."

"So what wouldn't I get?" I asked.

"People like that, they're trying to hurt me. When someone is ignorant on purpose, it's easy to not let it hurt. Because it's nothing personal. You should almost feel sorry for them because they're such idiots."

This conversation was quickly going places I didn't understand.

"But—"

"But nothing," Dakota said, cutting me off. He was definitely angry. "You sat here and asked what happened to my parents. Like you couldn't believe my parents would actually own a house like this."

"Yeah, but—"

"You couldn't believe that," his voice became a sneer, "a redskin would actually belong in a neighborhood like this. It's like you think that because of the way I look, my parents and I should live on a reservation somewhere, beating tom-toms and living in tepees."

He took a breath. "See, that's what hurts. Not when someone is ignorant on purpose. But when they're ignorant without thinking. It really gets to me, and I want to explode. For you to assume—"

"Shut your mouth," I said. I could feel my anger begin to match his. "Shut your mouth before I knock it shut."

"Sure," he said, "that's the only way you know how to deal with stuff. Hit and punch. We all know why you get traded around so much."

"You're the one who is ignorant," I practically shouted. "Asking about your parents had nothing to do with what you look like."

"Really?" He said it in such a way that I knew he didn't believe me. Nor did he care to believe me.

"Really," I said. "Most of the time mothers live when they give birth. And most of the time babies get to go home with their mothers. But not always. Not me. My mother died. So I didn't get to go home with my mother. Not that I had a home to go to anyway. Because my dad likes whiskey too much."

Now it was my turn to pause for breath. "The only reason I couldn't believe your parents lived in this house is because you made it sound like they weren't your parents. And I couldn't believe anybody I know might have it this good."

I turned the key in my ignition and floored the gas to get the car going. I didn't care how much noise it made.

"So why don't you get on a horse, Tonto," I said. My jaw hurt from how tight I was gritting my teeth. "Ride it on up to your nice home and your nice parents. This poor paleface will get out of here and quit embarrassing you and your neighborhood."

I didn't give him a chance to even get all the way out of the car. I popped the clutch and took off as he was stepping onto the pavement. He had to jump to get away from my car, and I roared off with my passenger door still wide open.

chapter nine

Two blocks later, I felt stupid. As cool air rushed into my car from the open door, I cooled down too. How was Dakota supposed to know how bad things had been when I was a kid?

If I had stopped to think, I would have probably understood why Dakota felt I had judged him because of his skin color.

But I'd let my temper get in the way. Worse, I'd said some awful things, really awful things.

My car door was banging back and forth, so I pulled over and stopped. I didn't move to shut the door though. I felt too sick about how I'd lost my temper. I wanted to bang my head against the steering wheel.

When I lose my temper, I lash out. Sometimes with my fists. Sometimes with my words. And later, when I think about it, I feel foolish. But I almost never apologize. I can hardly allow myself to think about some of the stupid things I do when I'm mad. How could I actually admit them out loud?

I banged the steering wheel. Not with my head. But with my fist. It didn't help.

The steering wheel was still there. My hand now hurt. And I still felt bad about what I'd said to Dakota.

That's when my car died. It sputtered and stopped, and my headlights dimmed. Before I left Saskatoon, a mechanic had told me I needed new electrical wiring. Naturally I had just laughed at the guy.

I wasn't laughing now. It was at least ten miles back to my billet's house. I didn't have enough money on me to call a taxi. It would cost me a fortune to have my car towed. And I sure couldn't afford to fix this heap.

I banged the steering wheel again. Then I shut off the headlights, got out of my car and walked around to slam the passenger door shut.

I sat down on the curb behind my car. Maybe if I pretended none of this had happened, it would all go away. The night sky had lightened slightly at the approach of dawn. I could almost see the outlines of branches above me. I felt totally alone.

I sat like that for five or ten minutes. Feeling alone was nothing new for me. I'd felt like that most of my life. This was worse though. A new day was ready to start, and it hit me that I didn't have much hope for anything. One more mistake and I was out of hockey.

I had no job, no money, no family. Dakota Smith, the one person who might have become a new friend for me in Seattle, was probably wishing I'd get run over by a train. I couldn't even walk back down the street and ask to use his phone. How could life get worse?

A vehicle approached from somewhere down the street. Its headlights swept the pavement under my car and bounced off my feet. With my luck, it would be a patrol car. The officers would take one look at my car and give me a ticket for littering.

I hunched down behind my car, hoping the headlights would keep moving and that whoever passed by would not notice me sitting on the curb.

The headlights did keep moving. The vehicle swept by, so quickly the driver could not have seen me. It wasn't a cop. I was ready to believe that at least one thing had gone right in the last half hour. Then I noticed the passing vehicle was a red 4x4 truck.

The brake lights glowed red as it slowed to turn onto the street where Dakota Smith lived.

A red 4x4 truck.

I flashed back in my memory to the truck that had almost hit Dakota's in the arena parking lot. A red 4x4 truck. Same make. Same model.

What were the chances of another truck, the same make and same model, cruising up to Dakota's house in the early hours of the morning?

Not very likely, I decided.

I forgot to remind myself that the last time I had seen a red 4x4 truck, the guys in it had a rifle. Without thinking, I was up on my feet and running down the sidewalk toward Dakota's house.

chapter ten

There were two. A pair of shadows. Each carried a baseball bat. They moved past where I was hiding behind the trunk of a large tree on the edge of Dakota's property.

I was glad to be out of their sight. I had to concentrate on breathing quietly as I tried to suck air into my lungs. I had sprinted here and was able to reach the house first because they had driven past me and parked well down the street. I considered jumping out and attacking them.

But when I spotted their baseball bats, I told myself I was interested in reaching my next birthday. I stayed hidden.

"You're sure the dog's on a chain?" I heard the bigger of the two ask in a low voice. In the half-light before dawn, I could see he had a beard and wore a lumberjack shirt.

"Yeah. The dog's on a chain. I was here yesterday."

They moved past. The second guy, also in a lumberjack shirt, was shorter and skinnier and was wearing a knitted cap. Along with his baseball bat, he carried a small, clear plastic bag. I couldn't tell what the bag held.

I went through my choices.

I could wait a few minutes until they were behind the house and then ring Dakota's front doorbell. That might give the guys a chance to get away though, as I tried to explain what was happening. Especially if the lights went on in the house as Dakota or his mother or father answered the door.

I could follow them and try to figure out what they were planning to do. But following them was useless, since I probably couldn't stop them unless I was prepared to let them know I was there. If I didn't give myself away, I wouldn't be able to follow them anyhow, because once they left the property, I wouldn't be able to keep up with their truck.

Thinking of their truck gave me the idea.

I waited until I was sure they had rounded the corner of the darkened house, and I sprinted away from the tree and back toward the street.

It took me less than a minute to reach their 4x4. They had parked it down the street and around a corner, in the shadows between two streetlights.

Perfect.

When I got close to the truck, I noticed a sticker on the window that warned the truck was protected with a security system.

I grinned. Even more perfect.

Now I knew exactly what I was going to do.

I searched for some tiny pebbles in the gutter beside the truck. I found four and put them in my mouth where I wouldn't lose them.

Squatting beside the front left tire, I unscrewed the small rubber cap from the tire's valve stem. I took one of the pebbles from my mouth and stuck it on top of the air valve. I screwed the cap on again. As the cap tightened, it pushed down on the pebble. The pebble pushed down the air valve. Air began to hiss from the tire.

Moving around the truck, I put pebbles into the three other valve caps. With all four tires hissing air, it seemed like the truck was sighing sadly as it began to settle on its rims.

I figured I would have to wait only another minute or two before I went on to stage two of my plan.

Unfortunately I didn't even get another ten seconds.

I'd been so worried that the two guys with baseball bats might show up, I hadn't stopped to think that anyone else might be awake at this early hour.

I glanced up and down the street, worrying about baseball bats. Instead I saw, down at the corner beside a fire hydrant, the outlines of two figures beneath a streetlight. A tall woman in a sweat suit and a big poodle at the end of the leash she was holding. The poodle was on three legs, watering the fire hydrant. The woman had one hand pressed to her head and was staring at me.

I doubted she would believe me if I told her the truck was hissing because it had a bad case of indigestion. I doubted she would believe me if I told her I owned the truck. Not if she had seen me mess around with the tires.

I made my decision.

I took a step away from the truck, ran toward it and rammed it with my shoulder.

It was such a heavy truck, it hardly rocked at all.

I took another step and rammed it again. Harder. The woman started walking toward me, hand still against her head.

What would it take to get this truck to bounce?

I hopped onto the front bumper. Holding the hood ornament to keep my balance, I jumped up and down on the bumper.

That did it.

The truck rocked, and the security system detected the motion. The headlights of the truck began to flash on and off. The horn blared at full volume.

Part two of my plan was now complete. I would have liked it if the tires were completely flat, but the woman and her poodle had forced me to act early. I was hoping cops would arrive at about the same time the men got back to their truck. With flat tires, the men with baseball bats would not be able to get away. If they got away on foot, the cops would still have their truck and be able to identify them from the license plate and ownership papers inside.

I would have loved to hide down the street and watch the action, but the woman in the sweat suit was waving at me, shouting at me to stop.

Lights began to flick on in the houses along the street.

If I didn't clear the scene, I'd have a lot of explaining to do.

I broke into a full run. I intended to circle the block, get back to Dakota's house, ring the doorbell, explain what had happened and let him or his parents go over to the truck and meet with the cops.

For the second time in less than a minute, the woman in the sweat suit wrecked my plans. Halfway down the street, I looked back over my shoulder as I was running. She had begun to chase me.

I almost laughed. She hadn't even taken her hand away from her head, and she figured she could keep up with me?

I ran harder.

"Stop!" she shouted.

I didn't stop. I was a WHL hockey player in the best shape of my life. Did she actually expect me to roll over and play dead?

I rounded the corner. My lead on the woman was so big she didn't have a chance at catching me.

Just as I congratulated myself on getting away, I heard barking. Not the yipping bark of tiny poodles, but a deeper meaner bark. I hadn't realized her poodle was so big.

I glanced back.

The dog's claws slipped and slid on the pavement as it rounded the corner at full speed.

Until that moment, I had thought I was running as fast as I could.

The poodle barked again. It was the size of a Doberman. Suddenly I discovered I had some extra speed left in me.

Still, it was a losing race.

A half block later, the dog caught me. I didn't see it catch me. I felt it catch me.

Its teeth ripped through the back of my jeans about where I'd normally sit. I knew I wouldn't want to sit for a few days.

The poodle dropped back for a second, getting ready to jump and take another hunk out of me. I veered from the street toward the nearest tree and saw a branch at head height. Without missing a step, I dove up toward it, grabbing it near the trunk of the tree. I pulled myself up, frantically kicking at the dog's jaws.

It is amazing how much more athletic you can become when you are scared out of your mind. I made it to a standing position up on that branch in record time.

The dog was below me, jumping up and scratching the trunk with its front paws. It wasn't barking, because my right shoe was stuck in its mouth.

The woman in the sweat suit arrived a few minutes later. When she got to the tree, I saw why her hand had been stuck to her head. She was carrying a cell phone. And speaking into it.

"Yes, officer," she said, her voice reaching me clearly. "I've followed him. He's here on Birchwood Street. Almost at the corner of Chestnut. You can't miss us. I'm standing in the street. He's in a tree."

She snapped the flip phone shut and clipped it on a belt around her waist.

"I always take a cell phone with me on my early morning jogs," she told me in a sharp triumphant voice. "You never know when it will come in handy."

Her poodle moved beside her and dropped my shoe at her feet. "Good dog, Orville."

My back end was bleeding, my lungs were raw from breathing so hard, the guys with the baseball bats were going to get away as the cops moved in on me, and to top it off, I had been treed by a poodle named Orville.

I could only think of one other time when my life had been worse. I'd cried then. I wasn't going to cry now.

Thirty seconds later, red and blue flashing lights bounced off trees and houses as a patrol car approached. Two cops stepped out of the car and walked up to the woman in the sweat suit.

The cops shone their flashlights in my eyes. All four of them stared up at me—two cops, the woman in the sweat suit and her big poodle.

At least I didn't feel lonely anymore.

chapter eleven

An hour later, I sat at the dining room table in the Smith house, staring at the most beautiful girl in the history of humankind. Early sunlight streamed in through tall windows. I had a cup of hot chocolate in my hands, a half-eaten omelet on the plate in front of me and a big lipstick smear on my cheek. Mrs. Smith had served me the hot chocolate. Mr. Smith had cooked the omelet for me. And the most beautiful girl in the history of humankind had given me a kiss.

"Mike, you can quit staring at her," Dakota said. His omelet was long gone, and he had finished a half loaf of toast. "She's only my sister."

"I'm not staring," I said, staring. "I'm listening. If Kendra wants to thank me again for saving her dog's life, it's only polite that I give her my full attention."

Kendra grinned at me. "Are you ready to tell us how it all happened? From the beginning. Right until you and the cops showed up at our door."

"Are you finished thanking me?"

"For now."

If I were her dog, I would have thumped my tail and run around in circles at the way she smiled.

I enjoyed staring at Kendra. Her hair was as dark as Dakota's, her skin a lighter copper. She wore her hair cut so it barely touched her shoulders. It hung straight and even and soft. Where Dakota's cheekbones were high and sharply visible, hers were high and rounded. Dakota's nose was strong and noble; hers was straight and perfect.

"My car stalled," I said. "As I was coming back here, I saw two men with baseball bats."

That was what I'd told Mr. and Mrs. Smith a half hour earlier in the presence of the cops. I didn't tell Kendra that I'd raced over from my stalled car, expecting to find the guys on the property. Kendra nodded, assuming that I had been coming over here to borrow the phone. She assumed that I had accidentally happened to see those guys. Earlier, the cops and Mr. and Mrs. Smith had made the same assumption. If they'd known I was coming over to find the guys, there would have been too many new questions. Like, how did I know to follow them? And until Dakota was ready to say something, I was going to keep my mouth shut about the part where Dakota and I had been shot at the day before. Whatever Dakota was hiding, it was still his business, and if he wasn't telling anyone, I didn't feel I should either.

"I know you did something to their truck," Kendra said. "I overheard some of what you were telling Mom and Dad."

"Yeah," I said. "I remembered a red truck going past my stalled car. I figured it was theirs, so when they went in the backyard—"

"They wanted to kill my dog," she said. "There were poison capsules in the steak in the plastic bag we found out there."

I nodded. She had already said this about ten times. But I didn't mind when she repeated herself. She figured I was the hero for waking everyone up before the dog ate the steak.

"What happened at the truck?" Dakota asked.

I explained, right down to the poodle chase. As I told the story, they both laughed. I squirmed on my chair once in a while and winced, hoping to get sympathy from Kendra for the wound I had taken in a tender area.

"Cool idea for letting the air out of the tires," Kendra said when I finished. "Where did you learn that?"

"Reform school," I said.

"Reform school?"

"For juvenile delinquents."

She grinned like I was joking. I wasn't, of course.

"The cops figure those two drove the truck away while they were chasing you." Dakota said it as a statement, not a question.

I nodded. "They had to have driven it on its wheel rims. They must have been desperate not to get caught."

"I wish the cops would have caught them." Kendra's dark eyes showed anger.

"How about you, Dakota?" I asked. "Wish they had been caught?"

He didn't show anything on his face. He locked eyes with me for a couple of seconds and shrugged his answer. "They're obviously crazy."

"The police think they're also the ones who burned your truck," I said to Dakota. We both knew they were. I wanted to see what Dakota was willing to admit. "The cops really want to find those guys."

"I find it hilarious that Mrs. Belford was the one who chased you down," Dakota said, "with her poodle."

He turned to Kendra. "Isn't her poodle named Orville?"

She nodded.

He turned back to me. "Mike, it would be a shame, wouldn't it, if the guys on the team knew you had been treed by a poodle named Orville. They'd never let you forget."

"A real shame," I said. "Good thing you can keep a secret."

"Maybe someday you can keep a secret for me."

"Good idea," I said. "Any secret you want, I'll keep."

Mr. Smith walked into the kitchen, followed by Mrs. Smith. I now understood a bit more about Dakota's family. Mr. Smith was a professor of archaeology. He'd been born and raised here in Seattle. He was not Native American.

He'd met his wife during some field research in tribal territory in the Interior of British Columbia, the province straight north of Washington. They'd fallen in love, gotten married and moved back to Seattle to the house Mr. Smith inherited.

"Well, Michael," Mr. Smith said, "why don't I give you a ride home."

"Thank you," I said.

"I've already arranged to have your car towed and fixed."

Mr. Smith must have seen my horror, which I was trying to hide.

"Yes," he said smoothly, "it's only fair that I take care of the expenses. After all, you did come to this household's defense."

I nodded. I was relieved because I didn't have much money. I told myself I would pay him back as soon as I could.

I stood from the table and backed away from Kendra and Dakota. I had no wish for Kendra to see the gaping hole in my jeans where Orville had done his best work.

"Visit any time," Kendra said.

I grinned. First chance I had, I was going to talk to Dakota and apologize for the stupid things I'd said. Maybe I could eventually come back and visit.

"If only you had remembered to take down their license number," Mr. Smith said as we stepped outside.

"If only," I said, knowing it had been a British Columbia license plate, 498 EAH.

Even if Dakota wouldn't go to anyone for help on this, I intended to do some looking around of my own.

chapter twelve

Mr. Smith dropped me off at my billet's house by 7:30 AM. Almost twelve hours later, I was at the rink, sitting in the dressing room with the rest of the team, waiting to step onto the ice for a home game against the Kamloops Blazers.

As we waited the final minutes to our 7:30 PM start, Coach Nesbitt informed us of something we all knew already from reading the sports section of the *Seattle*

Post-Intelligencer. The Saskatoon Blades had won their last five games. They were only two points behind us in the overall league standings.

Then Coach Nesbitt told us something we did not know. The Blades were ahead 5-0 in their game against the Brandon Wheat Kings. Because they were playing two time zones away, in Central Standard Time, it was nearly nine-thirty there. In other words, the game was all but finished. The Blades would certainly win.

If we lost tonight's game, then, we would fall back into a tie with the Blades. They were a hot team right now. We couldn't afford to give them the chance to take first place, not this late in the season.

I looked around the dressing room as Coach Nesbitt finished telling us how important it was for us to win tonight. Some of the guys were chewing gum. Some were staring at the floor. Some were staring at the ceiling.

I glanced down the bench at Dakota. He'd buried his face in his hands and was completely still. It was something I'd noticed him doing nearly every game.

"That's it," Coach Nesbitt said. "Get on the ice and show them what you can do."

Coach Nesbitt clapped his hands twice, his signal for us to get moving.

Dakota slowly lifted his face out of his hands.

I stood but didn't join the line of players trooping out of the dressing room. I let them pass. A few clapped me on the back. I was glad it was my back and not my rear end. It was still sensitive where Orville had sunk his teeth into me, and I didn't need a healthy slap to remind me exactly how sore it was.

"Go crazy, Crazy," one of our defensemen said. "Burn it up tonight."

I grinned in reply. "You bet."

Dakota was at the very end of the line. He didn't say anything as he moved by me. I followed him and the rest of the guys down the rubber mats in the center of the hallway.

The crowd cheered as, one by one, we stepped onto the ice.

I like this part of the game. I stepped onto the ice and blinked as my eyes adjusted to the bright lights after the dim hallway. I sucked in a few breaths of the chilled air. The ice surface shone, untouched by the gouging and cutting of skate blades. The crowd was loud and hopeful, clapping and yelling to the beat of loud music.

Hockey was the only thing in my life that hadn't let me down. Any mistakes in hockey were my responsibility. They didn't happen because someone else made a promise and didn't keep it.

I grinned with pleasure to be on the ice, circling our half of the end for last-minute warm-ups.

I matched Dakota stride for stride, gliding up beside him.

"Hey," I said, "let me ask you something."

"About this morning?"

"No," I said, "at the start of every game you put your hands over your face. What's the deal?"

He stared at me for a few seconds as if deciding whether to answer. Uniforms flashed past us as the other guys on our team skated harder.

"Prayer," he finally said, "that none of us gets hurt."

"Prayer?" I hadn't considered that.

His face tightened. "Yeah, prayer. You think I should beat tom-toms and chant to spirits in the sky?"

Not this again. Was it my fault he was going to take everything the wrong way? I opened my mouth to tell him he could stuff tom-toms in his ear. Then I took a deep breath instead.

"Dakota, I was out of line this morning with that Tonto stuff. I said it because I was mad. I'm..." I had to take another deep breath to get the words out. "I'm sorry."

He stared at me a few more seconds. We were still slowly skating around the boards. Other guys ahead and behind were matching our pace, having their own conversations. I doubted they were like this one.

"Mike," Dakota said, his face less tight, "you don't apologize often, do you?"

"This is the first time in as long as I can remember."

"I shouldn't have lost my cool either," he said. I was glad he didn't try to say anything to make me feel better about my mother. People always try to apologize when they hear about her. Which is stupid. It happened a long time ago.

"By the way," Dakota continued, "thanks."

"Thanks?"

"You could have told the cops more than you did about the guys in the red truck."

"Not a big deal," I said. "Besides, you haven't told anyone about Orville the poodle."

No answer from Dakota.

"Right?" I persisted.

He shrugged, grinned and put on a burst of speed to leave me behind. Ten seconds later, the referee blew his whistle to end warm-ups.

Orville the poodle.

I grinned and began to concentrate on the game ahead of us.

chapter thirteen

Almost halfway through the second period, we were down by two goals.

Two big goals.

The Blazers were a strong defensive team. They loved getting the lead, because then they would switch to a version of the neutral zone trap. They would only send one forward, not two or three, into our end to chase the puck. The good news was that it made it easy for us to move the puck out of our end. The bad news was that they would have four skaters waiting for us in the middle area of the ice, the neutral zone. It's tough trying to pass the puck around with that many skaters in the way. Nearly the only way to beat that kind of defense is to dump the puck behind them into their end and chase it down. Except that they kept so many skaters hanging back, a Blazer usually beat you to the puck. Even if you managed to get to the puck first, a Blazer would be right on you, checking you hard or knocking you into the boards.

Dakota and I sat on the bench, waiting for our next shift on the ice.

"Mike," he said as he leaned over, "you're the closest thing to a rocket I've seen in this league."

I gave him a strange look. Where was this coming from? And where was it going?

"What I mean," he said, "is that nobody can take off faster than you can."

"What you mean," I said, "is I've got short legs and they start faster than anybody else's."

"I wasn't calling you short."

"And I wasn't saying you needed tom-toms to pray."

He grinned. "I get your point. Maybe I could be a little less touchy."

"Something like that."

"It's a deal," Dakota said. "Now, let's get back to those short, stubby, fast legs of yours."

He explained something he wanted to try.

I told him he was crazy.

He told me that craziness was my department.

I agreed. Then I agreed to his plan.

The next face-off resulted from a Blazer offside, and the referee dropped the puck just outside our blue line. Dakota, at center, didn't fight hard to win the face-off. Instead he let the Blazer center knock the puck back to his defenseman.

As expected the Blazer defenseman fired the puck along the boards into our zone. Gary Niestrom, our goalie, was forced to step out of the net and skate behind it to stop it from continuing around the boards.

Dakota waved for the puck. Niestrom left it there for Dakota.

Because the Blazers only sent one skater in, Dakota was able to come out from behind the net unchecked.

The rest of the Blazers stayed outside the blue line, filling the neutral center ice area, guarding me and the other winger, and making sure we weren't open for a pass.

Instead of cruising the ice and trying to find an opening, I stood on our blue line along the boards, waiting for Dakota to bring the puck up the ice. Because I wasn't moving, I kept the Blazer winger and defenseman up the ice, close to me.

Just before Dakota reached the blue line, I bolted, trying to become the rocket Dakota said I was. I busted toward the center of the other blue line, aiming for the open space between both of their defensemen.

At first they didn't react. They knew I wasn't looking back for a pass from Dakota. They knew I wasn't even in the open for a pass—at least, for a pass along the ice.

I kept busting hard, hoping Dakota was doing what he'd promised. And hoping he would be as accurate as a quarterback. Just when I thought it was too late, I saw both of the Blazer defensemen look up toward the rafters.

I risked turning my head slightly.

And there it was. The puck, in the air, sailing down, over my head and over the heads of both defensemen.

I was already at full speed. They were just starting to figure it out. Dakota had flicked the puck in a high lazy loop over the entire center ice area and over all the skaters who clogged it.

The puck flopped onto the ice ahead of me. The Blazer defensemen cut into the middle to stop me. They didn't have a chance. I had a two-step head start, and they weren't even close to reaching my speed.

The puck wobbled.

I scooped it with my stick, still pushing hard on a wide-open breakaway. I moved in, faked a shot, pretending to make a move to the left. The fakes were enough to get the goalie moving, and his legs opened slightly. As I was bringing the puck back toward me, I fired a low wrist shot from the heel of my blade at the opening between his pads. The puck nicked the inside of the goalie's skate and bounced left, catching the inside of the post and tumbling into the net.

I raised my hands and stick in joy and wheeled in a big circle back to center ice.

Their left defenseman had just slammed his stick down in disgust at how we'd beaten them on the goal. I nearly hit him as I turned my victory circle and had to lean hard to cut around him.

He saw me out of the corner of his eye and gave me a straight-armed shove. Most times, it wouldn't have done anything to me. I'm low to the ice, and it takes a lot to knock me over. This time, however, I was leaning and off balance. His shove flipped me onto my back.

I hit the ice shoulders first. Then my head and helmet slammed onto the ice. If not for my mouthguard, my teeth would have smashed together, probably breaking a couple. As it was, I mashed my tongue good. My momentum sent me sliding into the boards.

For a moment, when I finally stopped, I stared at the rafters of the arena, trying to decide what truck had run me over. I tasted blood.

I started to get mad, but I didn't care. Nobody hit me with a cheap shot like that and got away with it.

I turned onto my knees and got to my feet, getting ready to charge as soon as I could find him.

There, over by the goalie.

I took my first step. And stopped. Not because I wanted to, but because someone had hold of my sweater.

I threw my arms back, trying to knock the person away from me.

I wanted their defenseman, and I wanted him bad.

"Let go," I grunted.

"Don't let him control you," Dakota said, refusing to loosen his grip.

Dakota put his arm around my shoulder and spun me around so I faced our players' bench instead of the defenseman I wanted to pound as hard as I could.

I struggled to turn back.

"Do not go crazy. Don't let him control you," Dakota repeated, leaning his face close to my ear. Fans screamed and yelled, and the noise seemed to shake the entire building.

Dakota was too strong for me, and I wasn't crazy enough to start swinging at my own center. Not yet.

"What are you talking about?" I screamed. "Did you see what the guy did to me?"

"Can't you figure it out? If you chase him down, then he just pushed your buttons. Do you want a jerk like him working you like a puppet on a string?"

"I want a jerk like him begging for mercy." I tried one last time to get free.

"You just scored a goal," Dakota said. "He just got a penalty. If you keep your cool, he'll be in the penalty box and you'll have a chance to score again. Isn't that better revenge than getting a penalty too?"

"Fine," I said. "Whatever."

I pushed away from Dakota and skated to the bench. Not only was I mad at their defenseman, but now I was also mad at Dakota for minding my business.

Coach Nesbitt grinned at me when I stepped into the players' box. "Great goal, Keats."

"Yeah," I said. My mind was on what I would have liked to do to their defenseman.

"And I'm proud of you for keeping your head out there." He gave my shoulder a few whacks. "You're making me look like a genius for trading for you."

My temper began to cool, and I allowed Coach's praise to sink in. It didn't feel that bad to have someone happy with me instead of disgusted with me.

Dakota slid in on the bench beside me.

"Thanks, bud," I said. "I owe you."

"Don't sweat it. We're back in the game."

And we were. Thirty seconds into the power play against the Blazers, our guys on the ice scored a goal to tie the game.

I jumped to my feet along with everyone else in the players' box.

My celebration didn't last long though.

Before any of us could sit down again, two cops in full uniform stepped into the box and motioned for Coach Nesbitt.

He joined them, and they had a whispered conversation. All three of them looked over at me.

I tried to figure out what I'd done wrong. I thought of Saskatoon and how it had been cops that delivered the bad news that got me kicked off the team. I bit the inside of my cheek and held my breath, expecting the worst.

Only it wasn't me they wanted. It was Dakota, who stood beside me.

They escorted him out of the players' box and led him away with more than half the game left to play. And he never returned.

chapter fourteen

I had just scored the overtime goal in the seventh and deciding game of the Stanley Cup finals. I was accepting cheers from adoring women in the crowd when Mrs. Olinsky, my billet, knocked on my bedroom door and woke me from my dream.

"Yes?" I croaked.

"Phone call," she said.

I rubbed my eyes. Phone call? The red digital numbers on my clock said 7:30 AM.

Who could be calling me at this hour on a Saturday? It couldn't be a family emergency. I didn't really have a family, and even if my dad decided he cared enough to call, I doubted he knew my number. Or even that I'd been traded twice since we last spoke.

I threw on jeans and a T-shirt and climbed the stairs to the family room. Mrs. Olinsky smiled. She was dressed and ready for the day. Her hands curled around a big mug of coffee. Mrs. Olinsky was always up early because she got up with Mr. Olinsky, who was a baker and had to be at work at five each morning.

Mrs. Olinsky winked at me as she handed me the phone.

I didn't understand her wink until I heard a female voice on the other end.

"Kendra?" I asked.

Mrs. Olinsky grinned, and I waved her away. She pretended to be mad at me as she walked out of the room.

"I'm really worried, Mike," Kendra said. Her voice sounded small and lost.

"Is it your dog?" I couldn't figure out why anyone wanted it dead, but maybe they had tried again.

"No," Kendra said, "it's Dakota. He's gone."

"Gone?" I said. "He can't be gone. The police wanted him to report every move he makes."

"That's what I told him. But he didn't listen. He's gone."

"What about your parents? What do they think?"

"My parents flew to Las Vegas for a weekend vacation. They don't know he's gone. All they know is what happened last night because the police called them at their hotel. They're flying back today."

"How much do you know about last night?" Coach Nesbitt had told us everything after the game. The players had all agreed to keep it secret. It made sense that Kendra knew, but if she didn't, I wasn't going to be the one to scare her.

"I know about the bomb threat," she said. "I know there was a phone call to the radio station saying that if Dakota didn't leave the game by the end of the second period, someone was going to blow up a bomb somewhere in the arena during the third period."

The radio station manager had decided it would be dumb to panic a crowd of thousands by announcing the threat on the air. He'd taken it to the cops, who in turn decided the best thing to do—lunatic as a bomb threat might be—was to take Dakota out of the game. The cops had then sent trained dogs through the stadium during the second period intermission, letting them sniff around for trace smells of explosives. The dogs had found nothing. The game had continued. None of us players knew this until the end of the game—which we won by a goal. Coach Nesbitt had told us as much as he knew and asked us to keep it a strict secret.

"You know about the phone call," I said. "What else?"

"Not much."

"That means you know something then," I said. "What?"

"Look," she said, "do you know where Dakota might have gone?"

"Me? Why would I—?"

"You're his friend. Maybe he told you."

"Friend?"

"He says great things about you. I was hoping you might know what this is all about."

"What what is all about? It sounds like you know more than I do."

"Mike," she said in the same small lost voice, "can we get together and talk about this?"

"Well...," I started to tell her that I was supposed to be at practice first thing this morning. For that matter, so was Dakota.

"It gets worse," she said, "but I can't tell you over the phone."

We arranged to meet at 8:00 PM at a convenience store near the arena. Because she lived so far away, we couldn't meet earlier. And I couldn't meet later. It was a Saturday, and Coach Nesbitt had a practice scheduled for 9:00 PM that night. I was supposed to be at the rink by 8:30 PM.

That didn't give us much time to talk. I hoped Dakota would show up at practice, and Kendra would be able to stop worrying right away. She sounded certain he would not and insisted only I could help her. Against my advice, she wasn't going to call her parents. Against my advice, she wasn't going to go to the cops.

Instead she was coming to me. And I knew nothing.

So, after I hung up the phone, I made the phone call I'd been putting off as long as possible.

I called the Royal Canadian Mounted Police detachment in Saskatoon, Saskatchewan, knowing it was a couple of time zones ahead.

"Captain Hummel, please," I said. I knew he worked the early shift. I hoped the cop answering the phone didn't recognize my voice.

"Hold the line."

I waited, counting each second. I'd promised Mrs. Olinsky I'd pay for this long-distance call. I didn't want to spend half of my call on hold. I also didn't like the suspense of waiting for what John Hummel might say when he found out I was on the line.

Ten, long slow seconds passed.

"Hummel," he said crisply.

"It's Mike Keats," I said. I held my breath.

I heard the sound of him letting out a big breath.

"Yes, Michael," he finally said.

It could have been worse. He could have hung up. Or lectured me again.

"I've never asked you for a favor before, have I?"

"You haven't," he said. "I don't think you've ever asked anyone for a favor. That's part of the problem."

"I'm asking now."

"This ought to be good," he said with a snort. "After the way you left and all."

"You're right," I said. This had not been a good idea. "I shouldn't be asking you for any favors. I'm sorry."

"Michael?"

"Sir, I'd like to say good-bye."

I set the phone down gently. My ears burned from embarrassment. Why had I thought he would help me?

I was barely back downstairs on my way to the bathroom to shower when the phone rang again.

I heard the low murmur of Mrs. Olinsky's voice. Moments later, she called down to me.

"Mike? It's a call from your old billet family from Saskatoon."

I briefly wondered why Captain Hummel had this phone number in Seattle. If it had not been because of caller ID, I realized, it would have been more surprising if he hadn't. I also realized he'd probably spoken to the Olinskys even before I arrived in Seattle, telling them what to expect about me.

"I'm not here," I said to Mrs. Olinsky.

"He warned me you would try that excuse. He says he's sorry."

I thought of John Hummel and his stern face. I thought of how he'd tried hard to make things right for me in Saskatoon. I thought he probably didn't apologize to kids like me very often.

I went back upstairs.

"Ask your favor, Keats," were his first words. "And now you just might get it. It was a bad time for a joke. I'm sorry."

I wanted to tell him that he was probably the person who had most treated me like a son. But I couldn't find the words.

"Captain Hummel," I said, "I have a friend down here who is in trouble. I'm trying to help him."

"Yes?" Hummel kept his voice neutral.

"Could you track down a license number for me?"

"Interested in trading information?"

I was sure John Hummel wanted me to tell him what had really happened the night of the high school dance in Saskatoon.

But I couldn't tell it to him back then—to him as a cop, or as a friend, or as my billet—and I could see no reason why this changed things.

"No, sir," I said. "I'm not interested in a trade."

"You can't blame me for trying."

"No, sir."

There was a long pause. I'm sure he was remembering the incident. Just like I was. If it hadn't happened, I'd still be in Saskatoon. John Hummel and I would still be speaking like friends, not like strangers.

"What's the license number?" he asked before the silence became hard to bear.

"It's a British Columbia plate," I told him. "Four-nine-eight-E-A-H."

"A British Columbia plate? Down in Seattle, Washington?"

"That's right," I said.

"Will you at least tell me what this is about?"

"I promise I will when I can."

"That's what you said about the high school dance."

"Yes, sir."

"You are a stubborn mule," he said. "That's probably why I like you, despite everything that happened here."

I grinned at the phone. "That's why I like you too."

"Very funny, Keats." Another pause. "I'll have it traced within half an hour."

"Thank you," I said. "I'll call you back later."

"Just remember, I'll be here when you finally get ready to talk about things."

I didn't reply.

"Hey, Keats," he said to break the awkward silence.

"Yes, sir?"

"Some of us in Saskatoon miss you."

chapter fifteen

"You're absolutely sure you want to do this?" I asked Kendra.

The Saturday evening practice had ended. Dakota had not shown up. Kendra and I were back at the convenience store, standing in the parking lot beside her red Miata convertible.

"Yes, of course I'm sure," she said. "If we take your car, we might break down halfway there."

"Hilarious," I said. "Absolutely hilarious. Why don't we stop by my billet's house? We can pick up the Corvette that I keep in storage there. Let's see, do I want to drive my red one today? Or my black one?"

"Don't get me wrong, Mike. I'm not trying to insult you or your car. It's just that we've got a long way to go and get back by my curfew. My car is the one we should take."

"That's not what I meant. Are you sure this is a good idea?"

"You told me the two guys in the red truck were from Lillooet, right? Your friend in the police force traced their plates for you."

"Yes, but—"

"While you were at practice, I went to a bookstore and bought a road atlas. I found out there's a dam near Lillooet. That's important because Dakota's cassette mentions a dam."

"You're actually going to let me listen to the cassette?" I asked her sarcastically.

During our earlier meeting, she had told me about it, but not what was on it.

"You are touchy, aren't you?"

I grinned. "Yup."

She grinned back. "Dakota didn't show up for practice. That's enough reason for you to hear it. Anyway, the other thing is that, according to the map, Lillooet is near where Dakota spends summers with our grandparents. It's got to be the place. So, yes, I'm sure about this."

"You know exactly what I'm asking. Not which car we should take. Not if we're headed in the right direction. But if it's a good idea to do this ourselves. I think we should call the cops." I grinned, briefly. "And believe me, I never thought I'd be saying something like that."

"Mike, once we're driving, I'm going to play the cassette for you. Then you'll understand why we can't call the cops."

"Your parents? What about them?"

"Look," she said, "I've been going over the road atlas. It's two hours to Vancouver. Another three hours to Carpenter Lake.

That gets us there by five this afternoon. We look around for an hour. Then we drive back. It gets us in Seattle by eleven tonight. You don't play until tomorrow night. On weekends, my parents want me home by midnight. I've left them a note telling them I'm out with a friend. So we have an hour to spare."

"But your parents should know about this. Wait for their plane to get in. Or at least leave a note saying where we're headed."

"You should listen to the cassette," she argued. "Then you'll understand."

I still wasn't ready. This seemed too crazy, even for me. She was sixteen, old enough for her driver's license and a car, but not old enough to step in for the cops.

I was seventeen. I'd driven here all the way from Saskatoon, Saskatchewan. I'd spent time in a reform school. I'd lived on my own for two summers. A five-hour drive into British Columbia wasn't a big deal. Except we were dealing with guys who shot rifles at trucks, burned trucks, tried to poison dogs and threatened to blow up arenas. I didn't like the situation at all. I pointed all of this out to her.

"It's only a five-hour drive," she repeated. "We'll go straight there and back. What can go wrong?"

Plenty, I figured, because plenty always seemed to go wrong in my life. I told myself to ignore her sad smile, to forget about how much I'd enjoyed it when she was happy with me for rescuing her dog. I told myself to finally do something sensible.

She threw me her car keys. "You drive," she said.

Call me Crazy. I ignored my own advice and got behind the steering wheel.

chapter sixteen

"Before you listen to the cassette," Kendra said, "there are a few things I want you to know about my brother."

I nodded but did not turn my head to look at her. We were headed north on Interstate 5, and traffic was heavy. I preferred Saskatchewan driving, where you saw another car only every five minutes. And I wasn't comfortable driving a new car. The scenery was tempting to look at—both the countryside and Kendra—but I needed to concentrate on the road.

"Ever since I can remember," she said, "Dakota's been serious..." She struggled to find the right words. "Not like he's totally serious, because he is funny and finds a lot of things in life funny."

"But he's serious," I said. I kept my eyes on the bumper of a Cadillac in front of me. "He thinks about things."

"Exactly. Dakota could have had a Miata too, you know. I mean, my dad inherited a lot of money. Dakota wouldn't take a new car. He said it was more important for him to drive what he could afford to buy himself."

"The old green truck."

Kendra sighed. "I think Dakota's right. He was always prouder of his truck than I am of this Miata. It doesn't really feel like it's mine."

She sighed again. "I love my brother, but he can drive me nuts with his thinking. I remember Christmas when he was eight and I was seven. Dakota asked Mom and Dad why he should believe in Jesus.

He said when he was little they told him about Santa Claus and Jesus. Since he knew Santa Claus wasn't true, he wondered if they had lied about Jesus too."

"Good logic," I said.

"Exactly. Like how are little kids supposed to know the difference? Same with Easter and Easter bunnies. And remember, Dakota was only eight. But Dakota has always been looking for answers. That's partly why he started calling himself Dakota."

"It's not his real name?" I gunned the car to squeeze into an open lane beside a semi. The Miata took off like a cat with its tail on fire. Maybe I wasn't as uncomfortable with a new car as I thought I was.

"His real name is Stephen. You know, of course, my mother is Native North American."

"I had figured that out," I said. "I didn't think your hair was naturally blond and that you dyed it dark."

She laughed.

"When Dakota was ten," she continued a few seconds later, "he asked to be allowed to spend the entire summer with our grandparents on the reservation where my parents met. Dakota wanted to learn more about his heritage."

"That makes sense."

"I don't look nearly as Native North American as he does," Kendra said. "I think kids bugged him a lot more in school."

I heard sadness in her voice. I risked turning my head from traffic to glance at her. She was staring out the window.

"Racism stinks," she said. "People decide they hate you without even knowing you."

I figured saying anything would be as useless as when people told me they were sorry my mom had died when I was born. I concentrated on traffic, waiting until Kendra was ready to go on.

"Anyway," she said a few miles later, "Stephen decided to be proud of his heritage. He started calling himself Dakota. And he started trying to learn more about tribal religion. That's what I mean. He's always been serious. When he was ten, he asked Dad to explain the meaning of life."

"Tough question. What did your dad say?"

"Dad said it was love and faith. Dakota said he would think about that. And he has, ever since."

I remembered how he prayed before each game. I mentioned that to Kendra.

She nodded. "He started going to church again with Mom and Dad and me. Just like that. Out of the blue around Christmastime. He's changed. Before then, he was tough, almost angry about life. But something changed him."

She hesitated and looked at the cassette. "I'm wondering if this has anything to do with it."

"You're taking your time playing it."

"I wanted you to know a few things about Dakota," Kendra said. "I wanted you to know that Dakota has been spending his summers in British Columbia with our grandparents—that he's learned to be proud of who he is—and that he's always been trying to figure things out."

"Meaning?"

"Meaning, before you listen to the tape, I want you to know that Dakota hung out with tribal elders and with some of the younger people on the reservation. Some of those people are just as angry about racism as Dakota is. I think Dakota figured they had the answers, just because they believed in their own answers so much."

"I don't get it," I said.

Kendra put her hand lightly on my arm.

"Mike," she said, "when you listen to the cassette, I don't want you to think the worst of Dakota because of who he chose as friends."

"I still don't get it."

"Remember I told you there is a dam on a lake near Lillooet?"

"I remember."

"On the cassette, you'll hear Dakota and his friends talking about the dam. It's called the Terzaghi Dam. On Carpenter Lake. They want to blow it up. Tomorrow."

chapter seventeen

I learned plenty by listening to the cassette, plenty that I didn't want to know. The first part of the tape was music. The important part was a conversation at the end. Dakota spoke a couple of times. Mostly though, it was people I didn't recognize. Some were excited voices. Some were angry. All of the discussion was about blowing up a dam on Carpenter Lake. The day they had picked was Sunday, tomorrow. That was the day the premier of British Columbia would visit

Lillooet to make speeches and look for votes in the upcoming election.

As the voices ended and the cassette began to hiss static, we passed a sign that informed us there were eighty miles left to the Canadian border. I wished we could turn around long before then. I wanted to return to a simpler world where all I had to do was worry about staying on the Seattle Thunderbirds hockey team. But now I understood why Kendra did not want to involve her parents or any cops. And why it was just going to be the two of us looking for her brother.

"You want to protect Dakota. Right?"

"I can't believe he would actually go through with this. But why would he leave early this morning unless he was still involved?"

I squinted as a ray of sunshine burst between a gap in the hills. I pulled the visor down and kept my eyes on the white lines that flashed by on the pavement.

"Kendra, tell me again what he said when he gave you the cassette."

She shrugged, a movement I caught from the corner of my eye. "He woke me up just before I called you this morning. He handed me the cassette and told me to give it to you as a present. He said he'd be back in a few days. Next thing I heard was the door closing, the garage door opening and him driving away in Mom's BMW."

"Why did you listen to the cassette if you were supposed to give it to me?"

"Remember when you were joking about your car the other day? How you said your radio didn't work and that you didn't even have a cassette player?"

I nodded. Over breakfast at the Smiths', when I was listing all the things wrong with my car, I'd told them about singing the entire drive from Saskatoon, just to keep myself company.

"Well," Kendra said, "I wondered why Dakota would give you a tape you couldn't use."

"I think I know why," I said. "He didn't expect me to listen to it. He just wanted me to keep it. It would be a safe place for it."

"I listened to it," she said. "It wasn't that safe."

"And there was a half hour of music at the beginning, right? He probably figured if you started it, you wouldn't listen all the way through."

Ahead of us, beside the road, was a highway patrol car. I held my breath until it was far behind us. Kendra and I were not breaking any laws. We were not doing anything wrong. Still, with this cassette in the car, I was nervous.

We crested a hill. I drove for a couple of miles in silence, deep in thought.

"This is what I think," I finally said. "Dakota is not involved. At least not the way you think."

I told Kendra about the rifle shots fired into Dakota's truck. I told her how he had refused to go to the cops about it. I told her about the same two guys showing up to poison her dog.

"I'm figuring they were trying to scare him into something."

"Into not blowing up the dam?" she asked.

I shook my head no. "The easiest way to stop that would be to go to the cops. They could easily arrest Dakota and the other guys on this tape."

"Then what were they trying to scare him into?" Kendra asked.

"Why would Dakota have this tape in the first place?" I asked her in return. "You think those guys taped their own conversations?"

"That would be stupid," Kendra said. "You heard what they were talking about."

"So it was taped secretly then, right?"

"That makes sense."

"It also makes sense that Dakota taped it secretly. After all, he had the tape."

"Sure," she said.

"If Dakota really wanted to blow up the dam, would he let you or me get hold of the cassette? If the dam blows, he could spend years in jail."

"I think I know what you're getting at." There was hope in her voice. "Those guys were trying to scare him into giving them the tape."

"That's the only thing I can think of," I said. "Dakota is trying to stop them from blowing up the dam. Maybe he was in on it for a while and changed his mind. Maybe he decided to get it on tape and threaten to expose them if they went ahead. They started threatening him to get the tape back. When he saw they were willing to kill your dog and willing to make bomb threats, he decided to leave town to make sure no one else would get hurt."

"That sounds more like the Dakota I know," Kendra said.

"There's only one problem." I noticed I was gripping the steering wheel so tight my knuckles were pale. "If Dakota did go up there, he went to try to stop them. These are not nice guys, Kendra. Dakota is in a lot of danger."

She didn't understand what I was thinking.

"And if Dakota is in danger," I said, "so are we."

chapter eighteen

At the Canadian border, traffic was heavy. We had to wait in line for half an hour to get through customs and into Canada. From there, we followed the Trans-Canada Highway east. The broad flat valley of the Fraser River began to narrow. By the time we reached a town called Hope, we were in the mountains.

I had been on this highway often, during road trips. Kamloops was ahead, and so was Prince George, home of the WHL Cougars.

On this trip, though, I wasn't sitting on a bus. I was behind the steering wheel of a Miata. On this trip, we wouldn't be taking the normal route on the wide, smooth, four-lane Coquihalla Highway into Kamloops. Instead at Hope, we turned north, staying on the Trans-Canada Highway, following the Fraser River upstream. This road too, led to Kamloops, but it was a far older highway and a longer route.

It was already three o'clock. We had roughly a hundred miles left—or, as the Canadian highway signs showed, a hundred and sixty kilometers. It was rugged, spectacular mountain country. This far upstream, the Fraser was a wild roaring river that cut through deep canyons. I was glad the skies were blue. I couldn't imagine driving this road in rain or snow.

Kendra and I talked about school and hockey. She told me funny stories about when she and Dakota were kids. We both did our best not to talk about the dam. It was like we wanted to pretend this wasn't happening. So we didn't talk about the plans we had made earlier. Once we got there, we intended to visit Kendra's grandparents first, to ask them if they had seen Dakota. If we couldn't find him that way, we'd drive the extra distance up to the Terzaghi Dam.

At a town called Lytton, we swung onto a narrower highway toward Lillooet. There hadn't been much traffic on the Trans-Canada. Most people took the four-lane highway because it was shorter and straighter through the mountains. Here, on the secondary road to Lillooet, there was even less traffic. It was five or ten minutes between vehicles.

As we got closer and closer to our destination, I began to realize how stupid we'd been to think we could do anything about this. We were basically in wilderness—huge mountains and hundreds of square miles of forest and rock with no roads except the one we traveled. How could we expect to actually find Dakota, let alone know what to do once we did? And what if we had guessed wrong? What if Dakota was still back in Seattle and needed our help there?

I kept my doubts from Kendra, though I think she had them too. The last dozen miles into Lillooet were very quiet.

"Gasoline?" she asked when the first buildings of the town appeared.

"Good idea," I said. "My turn to pay."

She didn't argue this time.

We pulled up to the pumps of a small service station. I stepped out of the Miata and yawned and stretched, my first good stretch since stopping at the border. A long-haired guy in blue coveralls wandered out and began to unscrew the gas cap.

"Fill it?" he asked.

I nodded yes.

Kendra came around from her side of the car.

"Mister," she said, "have you seen a black BMW today?"

He shrugged.

"This is the only road into Lillooet, right?" Kendra said. "There's not much traffic on it. I was hoping you might have noticed. It's a four-door black BMW."

He shrugged again.

Kendra looked at me. "Well, it was worth a try."

"Sure," I said.

Kendra and I stared down the road as we waited for the gas tank to fill. Lillooet was a small town—the map said less than two thousand people. It had a couple of hotels and a couple of restaurants, a small grocery store, weathered houses. Hills and mountains served as a backdrop.

I shivered at a breeze blowing through the valleys. It was colder here than back in Seattle.

Where was Dakota? What was he doing at this very moment?

"Forty dollars," the attendant said.

I counted out the exact amount of money and handed it to him. He hurried back inside, moving faster than when he had approached our car.

Kendra and I got back into the Miata. As I was pulling my seatbelt over my shoulder, I noticed the service station attendant was on the telephone.

I didn't think much about his hurrying back inside and getting on the telephone.

Five minutes later, on the other side of Lillooet, I had a good idea why he had. And I had a good idea who he had called.

Kendra had been right, of course. There wasn't much traffic on the road, and it was the only way into Lillooet from the south. It should have been very easy to spot a black BMW. Almost as easy as it would be to spot a red Miata.

We had just turned onto a gravel road leading into the hills. No other traffic. Just us in isolation.

Then a red 4x4 truck appeared in my rearview mirror.

"Kendra, I've got a bad feeling about this."

"Why?" she asked. "Remember, we're only going to spend an hour here. If we don't find Dakota, we go back."

"I hope so," I said. She'd find out about the truck soon enough. "I really hope so."

The red 4x4 had pulled up behind us. It filled my entire mirror.

The road was twisting and turning with trees on both sides. I couldn't see much ahead of us. I couldn't go much faster. Not on gravel.

"Are there any other roads ahead? Any place we can turn?" I asked.

Kendra still didn't know the front-end grill of the truck was almost touching the bumper of her car.

"No," she answered, "this road goes for about ten miles before we get to my grandparents'."

"Great," I said, not meaning it.

Strangely, the red truck backed off.

I wondered if this was good or bad.

Much as I was trying to concentrate on the road, I risked another glance into the rearview mirror.

I watched someone on the passenger side lean out of the truck. I hoped my eyes were fooling me. I hoped it wasn't a rifle he was pointing at the back of the Miata.

I hoped wrong.

The bullet came with an explosion from the rifle and a popping sound from the tire. The steering wheel jerked itself in my hands, and the back end of the car started sliding in the gravel. He'd shot one of the rear tires.

Kendra screamed. "What was that?"

The car lurched as it slowed. "An order to stop," I said. "And we don't have much choice about it."

chapter nineteen

The good news was that we found Dakota. The bad news was where we found him, how we found him and what he told us when we found him.

"No," he groaned as we climbed down a ladder, "this can't be happening."

"Hey, Dakota," I said. "Nice pad. Is the rent expensive? Do you get maid service?"

Kendra, shivering in her sweater beside me, did not make any jokes about our new surroundings. Although this was the first time I'd been kidnapped, I'd guess that most of the time kidnappers shut a door behind you when they dump you into a room. Our kidnappers—the two men from the red 4x4—had forced us to climb a ladder down into a room. And they shut the door above us.

It was an underground bunker. The hatch door at ground level was covered with sod, in a small clearing about a five-minute walk from a narrow road that stopped halfway up a mountain. Unless you knew exactly where to look for the clearing, you'd never find it. And once in the clearing, unless you knew exactly where to look for the door handle in the sod, you'd never find it, not even if you were standing on top of the door. From there, a round concrete tunnel—like an extra-wide manhole—dropped straight down. We had climbed down a ladder of iron bars stuck in the concrete. I had counted twenty steps down to the second hatch door, which opened to the bunker. The iron-bar ladder continued down the concrete wall of the bunker itself, letting us climb down to the floor.

And that's where Kendra and I stood—on the concrete floor, looking up at a concrete ceiling as a hatch door above us was closed and locked on the outside.

The room was square, maybe twenty steps across. The walls were undecorated concrete gray. A single lightbulb hung down, throwing harsh light. An old couch stood in one corner, a kitchen table in the center, a battered stereo system in another corner. A refrigerator filled one more corner. I also saw a small door in the far wall.

Dakota sat on the couch. He watched me check out the room. When I finally turned my gaze to him, he said, "It's their hideout."

"Really?" I said. My sarcasm was lost on him.

"How did you guys get here?" he asked.

"Your friends in the red 4x4," I answered. *Friends* was a term I used lightly here. A few days earlier, I'd seen them in the darkness when they visited Dakota's house. Today, on the road, I'd seen their faces. One had eyebrows that almost grew together. The skin above his beard was pocked with old scars from pimples. The skinnier one had a ragged scar across his chin; his face and eyes reminded me of a ferret. Both of them stunk like month-old body odor. I'd almost been happy when they shoved us down into the bunker; at least now I could breathe through my nose.

"I mean, how did you get here to Lillooet?" Dakota asked. "And why?"

Kendra explained. Dakota could only groan and shake his head the entire time she spoke.

"How long have you been here?" I asked him.

"Long enough to know there's nothing in here to help us escape," he said, "and only one way out. The hatch." He pointed upward unnecessarily. Kendra and I looked up. "It's made of three-inch steel. In a hundred years, we couldn't break through it."

Dakota caught me looking at a small door on the other side of the room.

"A toilet," he said.

"Any windows?" I asked.

He started to answer, realized I was joking and smiled.

"No windows."

"Any good guys know about this place?" Nobody could rescue us if nobody knew where to find us.

He shook his head no. "I didn't even know about it, and I thought I was real close to the top of this group."

Kendra moved to the couch and sat beside him. "What group, Dakota? What's this all about?"

He closed his eyes and rubbed his face. "I hardly know where to start."

"You spent your summers up here," I said. "Kendra told me you started visiting your grandparents when you were ten."

"Yeah. That's a good place to start. I made friends. I came back each summer and hung out with them. There were a few in the bunch who, like me, really hated the way things were for Native North Americans. We'd learned enough in history books to know about broken treaties. Stuff like that. I could tell you nightmare stories about entire tribes being wiped out from starvation and disease when the white settlers first took away their land. Worst of all, it seemed that the government wasn't willing to listen to our land claims."

"Land claims around here?"

"Land claims all across the country. In Alberta, they built the Oldman Dam without caring what we had to say. I could give you a dozen examples where Native protests didn't work: lumber companies moving in, hydro-electric companies taking over land. All that stuff."

I nodded. I didn't pay much attention to newspapers, but even I knew there had been times when these things made head-line news.

"Well," Dakota said, "last summer, it got more serious. My friends and I were always talking about how great it would have been if we'd been around to fight Custer.

Then a couple of the older guys recruited us. Most of the tribal elders would have nothing to do with them, but I didn't know that at the time. These few guys were promising big changes, if only we'd help them."

"Them?" I asked.

"Don't get me wrong, Mike. Lots of people around here grumble. But that's all they do. They know there're a lot of good things about life today too. They know they can't go back a couple centuries before white settlers arrived. They know life needs give and take. They're willing to work things through with the government. But there's also this fringe group. And I discovered too late that it's really weird about things."

"Weird?" Kendra asked.

"These rebels are psycho. Like the two who brought you here. I think they're using this whole race thing just to get a war started. They want to fight, just for the sake of fighting. I mean, look at this bunker. They want a battle. It's like the crazies who blew up the federal building in Oklahoma. Nutso. They have military training and everything. Only I didn't figure that out until it was too late."

"You realized it when they started talking about blowing up the dam?"

"Blowing up the dam is bad enough. Then they started talking about killing the premier of British Columbia at the same time. Tomorrow, when he gives his speech in Lillooet, a hundred square miles of Carpenter Lake is going to burst through the dam and come rushing down the valley. Even if the premier gets out in time, it will be close enough to murder to give them the press coverage they want."

"These guys are serious," I said.

"I knew for certain they'd kill me if I tried to back out. So I pretended to go along with them. I brought in a microrecorder and taped one of our discussions. Believe me, I was sweating. If they had found the recorder on me, I would have been cut into a hundred pieces and thrown into the woods as bear bait."

I nodded. "We listened to it on the way up."

He stared at me, his mouth dropping open in horror.

"What's the matter?" Kendra said. "I told you we listened to the tape."

"I thought you listened to it back in Seattle. If they find the tape in the car," Dakota said, "all three of us are dead."

"Dead?" said Kendra.

I couldn't say a word.

"I told you. These guys are psycho," said Dakota. "Once I made the tape, I waited until I was back in Seattle. I called them and told them if they did anything, I'd release it to the police. Since then, they've done everything short of killing me to get it back. And you know why they didn't kill me?"

It was my turn to groan and close my eyes and rub my face. "Because they were afraid of who might get the tape."

"Exactly," Dakota said. "Until now, it was a standoff. I didn't want to take the tape to the police ahead of time, because I had been part of the planning. These rebels couldn't do anything because if they did, they knew I would go to the police, no matter how much trouble it caused me."

"Why did you come up here?" Kendra asked. "I mean, it's like going into the lion's den."

Dakota took her hand. "They tried to kill your dog. They told me they would kill you next. Then Mom and Dad. I was hoping I could find a way to stop them. I mean, I got us into this mess. I was going to get us out. Having you give the tape to Mike was insurance."

"You said you used a microrecorder," I said. "But we listened to a cassette. You've got copies."

"I do. I transferred the discussion onto a cassette from the microtape. I added a half hour of music at the beginning of the cassette just in case anyone accidentally plugged it in a stereo. I buried the original microtape in the backyard. But that won't do us any good as backup."

"Why not?" Kendra asked.

"Because without you or me as witnesses, even if the police do get the original microtape, they'll have a tough time knowing where to start looking for the people whose voices are on the tape.

"They already told me that tomorrow, when that dam blows, I go with it." He bit his lower lip and corrected himself. "Now, I guess, we all go with it."

chapter twenty

What do you do the night before the morning you think you'll die?

You think a lot. You worry some. But mostly you don't really believe it's going to happen. I had my own reason to hope, but I didn't share it with Dakota and Kendra. It would be too cruel if nothing came of it.

To avoid thinking or worrying, we told funny stories. Stories that had happened to us or around us. Dakota and I told our best hockey stories, and our worst.

Still, time passed too slowly.

Sometime close to midnight, we decided we would try to sleep. The old couch pulled out to a bed. Kendra and Dakota took it. I used the cushions from the couch to make a bed on the floor. There were no blankets or pillows. We settled back and hoped the clothes we were wearing would be enough to keep us from getting too cold.

A few minutes after we shut the light off, Kendra spoke into the pitch black darkness.

"I don't like this. It's too dark."

"They've got candles in here," Dakota said. He turned the light back on, found the candles and placed one in the neck of an empty bottle. Then he lit the candle and set it in the center of the kitchen table before shutting the light off again.

The candle made a nice warm glowing light. It was almost cozy. If only dawn would never arrive.

After a few minutes of silence, Dakota spoke softly.

"Mike," he said, "let me ask you a personal question."

"Sure." Normally I don't like personal questions. But something about knowing you might die together makes it easier to open up.

"What happened back in Saskatoon?"

Kendra giggled. "He gave a guy a wedgie. A super wedgie. That was the best story you guys told all night."

I knew, however, that Dakota was asking about something that had happened before that game.

"What did you hear?" I asked Dakota.

"That there had been a 'discipline' problem."

"You heard right," I said. I half hoped he'd leave it at that. I half hoped he would continue. It might be nice to finally tell someone the truth.

"I don't get it," he said. "You've got a temper, and you get a lot of penalties. But you don't seem like someone who would hurt the team. And if you'd done something major, like break a guy's head with a stick, we would have heard about it. Besides, you'd nearly spent the entire season with the Blades. I mean, before that, you really bounced around the league. For the Blades to keep you, they must have liked what you were doing there."

I was on my back, hands behind my head, with my eyes open wide. A few minutes passed.

"I'm sorry," Dakota said. "I should have minded my own business."

"No," I said, "don't sweat it. I'm just trying to figure out the best way to explain."

I saw in my mind the first day I'd met my Saskatoon billet, John Hummel, a captain in the Royal Canadian Mounted Police. He'd given me a big, gruff hard handshake. He'd introduced me to his wife and son—Matt, a guy my age.

"Dakota," I said, "the reason I bounced from team to team was because I was trouble. I loved hockey. I hated coaches, assistant coaches, principals, teachers and anybody who told me what to do.

Saskatoon was different. My new billet..."
I struggled for a moment, because I'd hardly admitted this to myself, let alone out loud. "He became like a father to me."

"But I thought—"

"You're right," I said quickly. "My mom died when I was born. My real dad is still alive."

A few seconds of silence passed.

"It's like this," I said before either of them asked anything else. My dad was no one's business. "The day Captain John Hummel first shook my hand, he looked me straight in the eye and told me he knew my background, he even knew my juvenile record. He said it didn't matter. He said it was where a man was going that mattered, not where he'd come from. And John Hummel played fair. He never made a promise he didn't keep. He never made a threat unless he meant to back it up. He settled me down. I still had my temper, but I stopped looking for fights with coaches and teachers. Things were going pretty good."

"No kidding," Dakota said. "You're one of the top five scorers in the league. Saskatoon had a great shot at winning the league title until they traded you away. That's why it seemed strange that they—"

"Traded me away," I said. "Remember? A discipline problem. One that had nothing to do with hockey."

I told Dakota and Kendra what had happened. I didn't even like thinking about it. Early in February, thieves had broken into a fur store in Saskatoon, taking nearly a hundred thousand dollars' worth of coats. It had been a headline story on all the radio and television stations. I hadn't thought anything about it.

The next night, there was a high school dance. I'd picked up a few guys from the team in my Toyota, and we had cruised toward the high school. In Saskatoon, the Royal Canadian Mounted Police worked hard at cracking down on drunk drivers. Because of it, they often had what they called check stops—spots on the road where the cops stopped cars and checked the drivers to see if they had been drinking. They usually picked a spot around a corner or just over a bridge, where drivers wouldn't have any advance warning and be able to turn around. For high school dances, they also set up check stops on the road leading to the school.

The RCMP had made a point of letting students know the check stop would be there. That was John Hummel's idea. He'd told me he didn't want to catch and punish underage students who drank. That wasn't his style. He respected kids my age. He said he wanted them to know about the check stop, so they wouldn't drink and drive in the first place. If they knew a check stop was planned, they wouldn't do anything stupid.

So when we came around the corner and saw the flashing lights of parked police cars, I wasn't surprised. Or worried. I hadn't been drinking. Neither had my teammates. We knew it wasn't cool.

We pulled over and stopped. Through John Hummel, I even knew the cop who walked up and shone his flashlight into the car. He said hello, told us all that he was proud of the way the Blades were playing. Then he'd said that he needed to do a quick search of the car. He didn't want it to appear that he was playing favorites because I lived with the Hummels.

I walked around back to open the trunk for him. When I opened it, I was as surprised as he was. Fur coats, wrapped in clear plastic to protect them from dust and oil, filled my entire trunk.

I paused as I told this to Kendra and Dakota. The feeling of disbelief and horror I'd felt to see those coats hit me as if I was still there, looking down on them.

"I know you didn't steal them!" Kendra exclaimed.

"They radioed Captain Hummel to come down." I laughed softly into the semidarkness of the concrete bunker. "You know what, Kendra? Captain Hummel said the same thing. He wasn't going to believe I had taken those fur coats."

That was the exact moment I can remember thinking he was like a father to me. He took me aside and asked me how the fur coats could have gotten there. He hadn't assumed that because I'd spent time in reform school, I was the thief. He trusted me and believed in me.

"So why the discipline problem?" Dakota asked.

"Simple," I said. I unclenched my fists in the darkness. "I told Captain John Hummel I had stolen them."

"But–"

"But nothing," I said to cut Kendra off. I could feel tears in my eyes. A lump in my throat. I knew if I kept talking, I'd cry. Just like I'd cried alone in my car, driving down to Seattle after the trade.

"Look," I said, putting anger in my voice, "the coats were returned. John Hummel made a big deal about how nobody could prove in court I'd taken them, that someone else could have easily put them in my trunk. Circumstantial evidence and all that. They decided to just keep it quiet and ship me out. They gave me to Seattle as my last chance."

It made me sadder that, to the end, John Hummel had stood up for me. He'd made sure no charges were filed. He'd made sure I was traded, not thrown out of hockey. He was a stand-up guy. I needed to stand up for him now, as much as I wanted to tell Kendra and Dakota more, and as much as I wanted someone else to know what had really happened. Even if those someone elses were going to die the same time I did.

"That's the end of the story," I said. "I want to go to sleep."

But of course, I couldn't fall asleep. I stared at the candle. Too soon, morning arrived. The hatch door was opened again.

chapter twenty-one

At 10:00 AM, at gunpoint, Ferret Face and Eyebrows put us in a rowboat. It was connected by rope to a motorboat. They left us in the center of the rowboat, hopped into the motorboat and began to tow us toward the center of Carpenter Lake. We could clearly see the concrete wall of the dam. They towed us in a line parallel to the dam, directly toward the far shore.

As they towed, I could have jumped from the rowboat at any time. So could

Kendra or Dakota. But none of us would have been able to swim to shore. First, the two in the motorboat had rifles. If they wanted, they could shoot us as if we were crippled ducks. They probably wouldn't have wasted any bullets though.

Because, if I jumped from the boat, it would be like committing suicide. My feet were wired together. And my wrists were wired together in front of me. Not only had they wired them, they had also wrapped our wrists and fingers with duct tape, covering them completely, right down to the finger-nails. I'd swim only as far as an average piano. To make it worse—as Ferret Face had told us with a grin—the water was so cold I would be dead in less than five minutes.

I stayed where I was.

"This is not good," I said to Dakota above the *chug-chug* of the outboard motor.

"This is not good," he agreed.

Kendra shivered. I wished I could put my arms around her. I wished I could tell her everything would be all right.

Instead I kept my mouth shut and scanned the skies. I would hope for a rescue as long as I could breathe. I was tempted to tell Dakota and Kendra to look too. But it wouldn't be fair.

I saw nothing in the skies except cottonball clouds against blue. It was a beautiful early spring day. Hills rose sharply on both sides of the lake. Snowcapped mountain peaks rose in the distance. The lake water was flat, dotted with chunks of ice and snow from the spring thaw. Sunshine sparkled in the wake of our boats.

I scanned the skies again. The far side of the lake was miles away. Maybe any second a plane or helicopter would appear over those hills.

Nothing, of course.

Twenty minutes of slow chugging later, we reached the approximate center of the lake. The men in the motorboat cut the engine and pulled on the rope connecting both boats. We drifted toward them.

"Dakota," Ferret Face said, "are you sorry now you betrayed the brotherhood?"

Dakota stared through him.

Ferret Face laughed. "He'll be blowing up the dam anyway. Himself."

He brought out the end of another piece of rope and tied it to a ring on our bow.

"It's like this," Ferret Face said. With both hands and a grunt, he lifted a plastic capsule. It was the shape and size of a watermelon, and it was attached to a coil of rope. "There's a current here. It will pull you toward the dam."

He held the watermelon-shaped plastic capsule over the boat's edge and lowered it gently into the water. It sank slowly, giving him enough time to let out the coils of rope attached to it. A few minutes later, nearly all of the rope had disappeared into the depths of the lake. As it reached the end of the rope, I understood. It was the rope he had just tied to our rowboat.

"Sixty feet," Ferret Face said. "Six stories down. Just waiting to bump against something. Like the dam you will hit in about fifteen minutes. And there is a series of underwater bombs attached to the dam by

suction cups. This bomb will trigger them
all. There's a couple of sensitive springs
that will make a connection and then"—he
grinned—"kaboom! The dam will go!"

He wagged his finger at Dakota. "And
you, my young traitor, will go with it."

Ferret Face grinned again. "And to
think, I have the Canadian government to
thank for all my fine training in military
explosives." His grin became a snarl. "Now
they can pay for my training again. The
hard way. This lake will hit the town like
a tidal wave two hundred feet high. Bye,
everyone."

"Cut the chatter," Eyebrows said. "Do
you want to be on this lake when the dam
goes? As it is, we're cutting it close."

"Yeah, I hear you."

Ferret Face grabbed a fishing rod from
his boat and clipped it upright in a holder
at the back of our rowboat. He did the
same with two more fishing rods.

"There," he said. "Just in case anyone
sees you from a distance. It will look like
you're trying to get some spring trout."

Ferret Face took a knife from his pocket and sliced us loose. He pushed the rowboat away and waved at us as they roared off in the motorboat.

We drifted toward the dam. Our hands and ankles were bound and useless. And we had a bomb, like an anchor, hanging six stories below us in the silent water. When it went off, we'd be dead. The premier would be dead. The town would be dead.

I looked into the skies again. Where was help?

"How can you be so calm?" I asked Dakota.

"You're not yelling and screaming," he pointed out.

"Inside I am."

He smiled. "Mike, you can't control life. It happens around and to you. Good and bad. What you can control is your attitude toward it. There's little we can do right now. But I'm going to control what I can: me."

Then Dakota did something that surprised and impressed me. He prayed quietly for all of us.

When he finished, he caught me staring.

"Faith," he explained, understanding my silent question. "It's being sure of the things you hope for. It's knowing something is real even when you can't see it. It took me a long time to understand that. Too long. Turning away from a plan to blow this dam up turned me back toward everything Dad has always tried to explain."

John Hummel had often talked to me about faith too. Because it had been John speaking—someone who lived up to what he said—I'd listened and tried to understand.

It's knowing something is real even when you can't see it. I was scared to the point of dry throat and heaving stomach. Being sure of things you hope for. Scared as I was, after Dakota's prayer, I did feel hope.

I looked over at Kendra. She was smiling, trying to be brave.

"I'd hold your hand if I could," I said.

"I'd let you," she said.

There seemed little else to say. We all stared at the dam as we drifted closer.

Five minutes later, we were close enough to the dam to see pieces of ice stuck on the dam wall. The ice clung to the concrete high above the water level, showing how the water had dropped during the winter as it flowed from the dam. At the rate we were drifting, I guessed we had ten minutes left.

"Can I tell you guys something?" I asked.

The sound of my voice seemed to startle them.

"Sure," Kendra said.

I think I knew why I wanted to talk. I was sad. Too soon, I'd be gone. I wanted to be able to tell someone how I felt about my seventeen years.

"Life is unfair," I said. "Not once in my life has something turned out right."

"Mike—"

"Let him talk." Dakota interrupted his sister. Maybe he understood the expression on my face.

"My mom died in the hospital when I was born. My dad liked to drink. How does a person have a chance with a beginning like that?"

I wasn't expecting an answer from either of them. "I want to tell you guys about the first time I stole a car. I was twelve."

Kendra's eyes widened.

"See, my dad, he never wanted to have anything to do with me. He kept shuffling me from relative to relative. I can remember each time he left me with someone new, he'd tell me that he loved me and that he had to do it because Mom was dead, and I'd think it was my fault and I deserved to be left alone. Sometimes it took him months to get back. I was a nice polite kid. I never gave anyone trouble. I wanted my dad to know I wouldn't be trouble for him either."

I stared at the dam. It was the length of a couple football fields away.

"The summer I was twelve, as soon as school was out, he took me to an aunt and uncle who lived on a farm. This time, though, he didn't just tell me he loved me, he bought me a horse. Just for me. He told me it was a present for never complaining. He told me when he came back next time, he'd try to find a way for us to stay together."

My eyes were dry. My throat was free of lumps. I thought this would be hard to talk about, but it wasn't. It was like I was talking about someone else.

"I called the horse Lucky. Dumb name. But I was only twelve. Every morning, even before the sun was up, I'd be out in the barn feeding Lucky. Grooming Lucky. I could hardly believe he was mine. And during the day, Lucky and I would go for long rides, and I'd tell him how great things were going to be when my dad came to get us. That horse and me, we were buds."

I thought back, remembering how I'd woken up each day of that summer, just grinning to be alive. I thought my happiness would never end. I had a horse, and my dad was coming back for me so we could be a real family.

"During meals at my aunt's house, I'd sit in the kitchen where I could watch the driveway that led up to the farmyard. In the living room, same thing. I'd take the chair that let me see outside. Even when I was watching television, I'd still keep an eye out for my dad's pickup truck."

I remembered the giant thrill I'd felt the evening that Dad's pickup turned into the driveway. I'd jumped from my chair and yelled and run out of the house, just bursting to show Dad everything Lucky and I could do together.

Now the dam was a football field away. How much time left? Eight minutes? Seven?

I thought of how I'd been forced to talk to a dozen psychologists during my times in reform school. Not once had I told this story. Now I didn't want to die until I got it out.

"So one night Dad finally pulled into the driveway," I told Kendra and Dakota. "Sure enough, there was a horse trailer behind his pickup truck. I went running out and—"

I stopped. My eyes weren't as dry as I wanted them to be.

"He drove right past me," I said. "Didn't look. I was waving like crazy, and he didn't even look. He drove up to the barn. I yelled and shouted when he got out of the truck, but he didn't look back. He just kept walking into the barn. When I got there, he already had Lucky out of the stall and was leading him into the horse trailer. Dad wouldn't answer my questions. Wouldn't say anything. Not until the horse trailer door was closed and he was ready to get in the truck again. Then he looked at me and—"

I took a deep breath. Kendra and Dakota were silent. I didn't dare look at them. I was afraid I'd see pity. I didn't want pity. I just wanted to get this story out of me.

"And he told me he had some gambling debts to pay and the horse would cover most of them. He said life wasn't fair, and I was stupid if I thought it was. And he drove away with Lucky and left me there alone."

I stared at the dam. I wondered if getting blown up would hurt. Or if it would happen so fast I wouldn't know it had happened. "That night," I said, continuing my story,

167

"I ran away and stole a car. It took the cops a week to find my dad for the court appearance. The judge let me out, and I stole another car. And another. I didn't care about being good anymore."

In another minute or two, the boat would be close enough to throw rocks and hit the dam. If we had rocks. If our hands weren't wired and taped. Five minutes left?

"Mike?" Kendra's voice was shaky.

"Don't sweat it," I told her. "It's not a big deal. I just wanted to tell someone."

"Guys!"

Dakota's voice wasn't shaky. It was excited. "Guys! Look!"

We looked. Above the lake, coming toward us, was the dark outline of a helicopter! Thirty seconds later, its sound reached us.

I glanced over at the dam. If the chopper kept moving at the rate it was, we'd have enough time.

The outline of the chopper grew. It was dull green. A Canadian Armed Forces chopper. Big. With twin engines.

Somehow I managed to stand, trying to show them my hands were bound. That way they'd know the fishing rods were decoys.

The chopper moved in close, beating wind down on us and rocking the rowboat.

"Get us away from the dam!" I shouted.

It was useless. The engine's roar was so loud it whipped my voice away.

"We see you!" It was a bullhorn coming from the chopper. A man was standing at the edge of the open cargo door, looking down on us.

I grinned. Captain John Hummel. Rescuing me again.

"We are radioing for men to reach you from the dam!" John Hummel said through the bullhorn. "Hang in there another ten minutes!"

Ten minutes! Ten minutes! We'd hit the dam in less than five. When we did, everything would blow. Including the chopper above us.

"No!" I screamed. "Now! Drop a ladder now!"

John Hummel waved and gave me a thumbs-up.

They had less than five minutes to tow the boat away. And they wouldn't if they thought everything was fine down here.

Dakota was right. There was plenty in life a person couldn't control. I often lost my temper because of it. This time, however, I was going to control the one thing I could in this situation. Me.

I knew the coldness of the water could kill me in less than five minutes. But so would the exploding dam. With my hands tied in front of me, I wouldn't be able to swim that long anyway, so five minutes didn't matter. What really mattered was getting someone from the helicopter down here in less than a minute. I didn't see any other way to get their attention.

With John Hummel watching, I dove over the edge of the rowboat into the black, cold water.

chapter twenty-two

The water sucked every bit of warmth from me as I flailed with my tied wrists and tied ankles. Twice I went under, sputtering for air each time I managed to get my head above water again.

After rising twice, it seemed I couldn't swing my arms as hard. My legs were heavy. I was sluggish, and my sodden clothes were taking me down.

"No!" I roared. But the water rose above my chin for the third time. Above my mouth. I closed my eyes as I started going down.

Something grabbed the back of my shirt and lifted me.

I found air again.

"Wrap your arms around the ladder! Hear me son! Wrap your arms!"

John Hummel was holding a rope ladder with one hand, dragging me with the other. He pulled me toward the bottom rung.

I managed to get the crooks of my bent arms through the rungs. The chopper started to lift us.

"No!"

"What!" Hummel had his mouth almost against my ear, shouting to be heard.

I turned my head. "Boat! Bomb!"

"What!"

"Grab the boat! Get them to tow it away from the dam! Bomb on the boat!"

He finally understood. With me clutching the ladder, he could hold a rung with one hand and wave upward with the other.

Slowly, painfully slowly, the helicopter moved us toward the boat according to his one-handed directions.

Hummel got his free hand on the cut piece of rope attached to the front of the boat. He lifted his hand briefly to wave the helicopter away from the dam, then grabbed the rope again.

Slowly, painfully slowly, we edged away from the dam. Dakota and Kendra were still in the boat. John Hummel held the rope ladder in one hand, the boat rope in the other.

"You're crazy!" Captain Hummel shouted in my ear. I was wrapped in a blanket, shaking hard. But it didn't matter how cold I was. I was alive. So were Kendra and Dakota. We were all in the cargo area of the chopper. "Jumping in the water was totally crazy!"

A soldier in uniform had a pair of wire snippers and worked at cutting us loose.

I nodded. I was crazy. But all of this was crazy.

Below, dangling from the helicopter's rope ladder, was the aluminum rowboat. Below the boat, dangling from a rope, was the watermelon-sized plastic capsule. And far, far below that, the tips of trees could be seen on the edge of a mountain, well inland from the lake. After John Hummel had carried each of us up the ladder—one by one, over his shoulder—the helicopter had risen straight up from the lake, making sure the bomb dangling from the boat had cleared everything. In a few minutes, when we had climbed high enough to keep us out of danger, they would drop the boat and the bomb to let it explode harmlessly against the rocks below. Even as we flew, trained military divers—dispatched by the chopper radio—were getting ready to fly to the dam and search for the bombs still attached by suction cups to the concrete dam.

"Mike," Dakota shouted over the chopper noise.

"Yeah?" I shouted back.

"How did they know to look for us?"

"Easy. I told them to." Dakota frowned, unable to understand.

I shrugged. I'd tell him later. Yesterday, during our stop at customs at the Canadian border, I'd told Kendra I had to go to the bathroom. Which I did. But I'd also made a phone call, telling John Hummel everything I'd heard on the tape, and as much as I knew about the situation. From the moment I'd heard the cassette conversation about blowing up a dam, I'd known this was something Kendra and I could not do alone, no matter how much she wanted to keep people from knowing what her brother had been involved with.

After all, I'm only crazy. Not stupid.

chapter twenty-three

Ten days later, the Thunderbirds were in Saskatoon to play the Blades. It was our last game of the regular season and the most important game of the season for us. We were tied with the Blades. The winner would take first place and have an easy run through the first two rounds of the playoffs. The loser would take second and struggle every single game after, just to stay alive in the playoffs.

Important as the game was, however, I was relaxed—more relaxed than I had ever been. I wanted to win, but I knew a simple secret. If we lost, I'd still be alive.

Maybe life had its rough spots. Maybe I'd gone through rougher spots than a lot of people had. There was nothing I could do about that, in the past or in the future. All I could control was my own attitude. And after facing the dam and expecting to die, I had plenty of questions, like the ones Dakota was asking about life. I'd ask them too, with an open mind. John Hummel would be proud of me.

After the dam, I'd found a lot to be grateful for. Even little things, like drinking a cold cola after a hard workout, laughing at dumb jokes in the dressing room and feeling the wind in my face as I busted up ice to the roar of a hockey crowd, were more important to me.

Of course, big things would be nice too, like winning important hockey games.

For this one, Dakota was back at center. He'd missed some playing time as he worked with military officials on both sides of the border. They'd promised him no legal trouble if he agreed to help them look for the radical militants responsible for plotting to bomb the dam.

He and I were playing a great game against the Blades. He'd scored two goals in the first period. I'd scored one in the second. We rocked during the third, not scoring but each hitting the goalpost twice during the first fifteen minutes of the period.

The clock showed five minutes left. We were up by a goal. Not much to relax on, not against the Blades in their own building.

Dakota got ready to take the face-off in our end, right side. I skated beside him.

"Here's the deal," I said quietly. "All you have to do is win this face-off. Get it back to Sharkey."

"Then what?" He grinned.

"Just do it," I said. "You'll see."

I skated into position. I'd already told Sharkey to give it a try. If he got the puck,

I wanted him to fire it along the boards behind the net, up the far side of the ice.

It became one of those few times that a plan works perfectly. When the ref dropped the puck, Dakota managed to slap the puck to Sharkey, back at the defense position.

Instead of taking the puck behind the net and waiting to find an open man, Sharkey spun around and slammed the puck. It followed the curve of the boards around the ice.

I was breaking hard for the far boards, toward a spot just outside of our blue line.

I caught their defenseman by surprise. The puck also caught him by surprise. It bounced past him to where I was already sprinting up the ice at full speed. I scooped the puck with my stick and raced toward their goalie—with no one between us! A breakaway!

I busted up ice as hard as I could. Their defenseman was doing the same as he chased me. Ten more steps and I could shoot.

I knew their guy was behind me and closing in. I knew I couldn't hold on much longer. Instead of moving in to stick-fake the goalie, I fired a long wrist shot. It was an awful shot. I was off balance and didn't do much more than give the goalie an easy marshmallow to catch waist high.

I slammed my stick onto the ice, disgusted with myself. How could I have missed after all that work to get the chance?

Someone pushed me from behind.

I spun, instantly ready for trouble.

It was John Oxford, their right winger. I knew him well. I'd played on the Blades with him most of the season, and he had a reputation as an enforcer. He's not much good with the puck, but he's a great fighter—someone who would fight better players on the other team to draw them into penalties and get them off the ice.

"Hey, loser," he said.

"Don't talk to yourself in public," I said. "People will think you're weird."

His face twisted into an ugly grimace. "Yeah?"

He punched me in the face.

Ten days ago, even knowing what he was trying to do, I would have lashed out and punched him back.

This time I smiled. I wasn't going to let him control my actions. I could do more for the Thunderbirds from the ice than the penalty box.

He punched again. It rocked me onto the back of my skate blades.

"Once more," I said. "Last chance. Ref's almost here to break it up."

He brought his hand back. I saw it coming. Slow. But I let him hit me. I took it on the side of the head. I shook it off.

I smiled again. No fury. It was almost fun, watching someone else lose his cool.

He moved to throw the fourth punch, but I'd guessed right. He only had time for three. The linesmen moved in on him and wrestled him to the ice.

He took a major five-minute penalty, leaving the Blades short-handed for the rest of the game. We didn't score. But we didn't have to. Our one-goal lead stood, and we left the ice as league champions.

After I showered and dressed, I shouldn't have been surprised to see John Hummel—leather overcoat over his police uniform—in the hallway outside our dressing room. After all, he lived in Saskatoon. And we really hadn't talked since our helicopter ride. Too many things had happened then.

"Hey, Michael," he said.

"Hey, Mr. Hummel. How are you?"

"Glad to see you," he said. He offered his hand, and I shook it.

It was good to see him. I owed him a lot.

"Mike," he said, "why don't we move down the hall where we can have some privacy."

Players were coming out of our dressing room in ones and twos. It wouldn't be a problem to move away from the door.

"Sure," I said, although I didn't know if I was sure. His voice was different, like he had bad news for me. Maybe after all this time someone had decided to lay charges on me from the fur store robbery. It would be just like John Hummel to take the hard job and face me directly instead of sending someone else.

I set my equipment bag down and followed his wide shoulders until we reached a quiet spot in the hallway.

"Last chance," he said, smiling sadly. "Tell me about those fur coats in your car."

"I stole them."

"We both know you didn't."

The way he was looking at me—pain in his eyes—made me wonder. Did he too know who had taken those coats?

"As you know, I never believed you," Hummel said. "I've stayed on this case ever since you left Saskatoon."

He paused, staring me straight in the eyes. "I've sent a memo to my commanding officer, asking him to relieve me from the case."

"Sir?" I felt sick for him, knowing before he told me what he meant by that.

"Conflict of interest," he said. "No father can or should investigate a crime involving his son."

I should have known John Hummel would eventually find out. I'd known myself, the instant I saw those coats.

His son, Matt, had a set of spare keys to my car. He could have easily borrowed it the night of the robbery while I was sleeping. And the next evening, Matt had been scared to the point of panic when I'd mentioned during dinner that I'd be driving to the dance. Matt had pulled me aside after dinner and tried to talk me into getting a friend to pick me up. Then he had begged to borrow my car, even when I told him my friends were depending on me to pick them up for the dance. I hadn't understood Matt's panic until later, when I'd opened the trunk with the cop watching. Then I'd understood who had put those fur coats in my trunk. I'd kept my mouth shut. I'd also promised Matt the next day if he did anything like that again, I'd spill everything.

And now I was staring into his father's face. There was terrible pain in John Hummel's eyes. But he wasn't running from it. Whatever happened, it was how you dealt with it that mattered.

"Mike," he said, "thanks for trying. I know how much it cost you to keep your mouth shut. I'll see to it your record is clear."

With that, John Hummel walked away. A step later, he stopped and turned back to me.

"Oh, and by the way—"

"Yes, sir?"

He grinned. "You should have scored on that breakaway."

"Hey." I grinned back. "We won. You can't expect life to be totally perfect."